EDUCATION

FROM THE BOTTOM

2D vs 3D

KAITLYN THOMPSON

E.F.T.B.

CHAPTER I

COIN DROP

Hello!

Can anyone hear me?

Can anyone just give me five minutes to talk?

I have deconstructed my cry for help by writing 3 different posts, describing my emotions in three different attempts.

Three!

I have even reposted a song that is subliminally singing out each painful emotion that is running through my entire body.

I even posted a selfie of a "weak" smile. Just a subtle lifting of the cheekbones so everyone will know I am not at my happiest potential.

I added a meme of a black and white photo of an ocean and a quote over it that is screaming, CHECK ON ME.

I have gone on my liking strike which means that I have not double tapped anyones posts because well hello!! I'm not doing all that good.

Yet no one seems to care one bit or notice any changes in behavior.

Well, I don't want to start my book off with being extremely dramatic, so I wouldn't say "no one" cared. I received maybe two "hey girl are you doing okay?" alerts, but they were from random followers. No one close to me, no one in my "circle".

Okay, maybe I am still in my dramatic mood. The ones closest to me are probably just assuming that when they see me later, they can just ask me about my posts then. Yeah that's it.

But then later came.

No concerns were brought up.

No one seemed to care.

Yes I know, here I go being a little over dramatic again. I am hurting within, and even with so many people around me I am still feeling extremely alone. I know I have started out this book with a very dramatic tone, but when you reach your last straw, well how else do you get your feelings out? You POUR them out. Anyways back to my rant. Maybe my people just haven't come across my posts yet. Maybe it is just that simple. They overlooked my post or they never even scrolled past it or something. Oh wait, they did. I see the eye icon symbol with their username on the list of followers who viewed it, and now it is evident that they did. As I look back up from my phone, I slowly scan the room full of all of my loved ones.

My heart beats in my chest, I can feel the rhythm as it pounds in my chest. One two, one two, one two. It's simple, this beat. The pulses of my heart. The little beat of the drum that controls my life, the one which seems so identical to the pulse of the 'like' button when someone double taps on a post. I feel the life inside of me screaming for help, as the pulse of my last post sits lifeless with no double taps, no beating hearts, no recognition, no likes.

Kaitlyn Thompson

Family members chatting and laughing, others fully engaged in their own devices with an expression on their face like they just found out how to cure world hunger. Young ones playing games which require little to no skill to win level to level until they realized the only thing that they did lose was their family time with their cousins. Everyone is all so busy doing their own, whatever. Everyone around each other and yet no one is together anymore. At this very moment, I am so down, and I would just feel that much better if someone took time to listen to me. But I understand. We are all too busy staying on top of the irrelevant business of individuals who exist in a world that seems more important than the people who are sitting right in front of you on the couch just praying for 5 minutes of a listening ear to just ease the pressure of all the thoughts that are hurting their mental health. I guess the subliminal messages and the weak smile wasn't enough of a red flag. I guess in order for me to let the ones around me know that I am not happy, I will have to use my handy dandy yellow circle emoji friends to express my emotions. Yes that will have to suffice.

Coin drops, the sound of an alert has lit up my iPhone screen. It calls for my undivided attention at that given moment. I opened it. A comment from my sister as she sits across the living room from where I sit, writing on the photo of my subtle smile, of my cry for help, of my efforts to find a listening ear, and she writes:

"Love the hair, girl".

* * * * * * *

We have lost sight of what disconnected really means. We believe that disconnecting is only occurring when we find ourselves too deep in a scroll, or realizing we burnt a dessert in the oven because we got lost in someone's live video, or just having that "okay i need to put my phone down and disconnect for a moment" moment. Well in reality ladies and gents, we are all becoming more and more disconnected with one another with or without the phone in our hands. We may think that this virtually advanced world has brought us all closer in humanity, but we are the most disconnected with one another than we have ever been before. Let's dive into this concept. Not for a short while, but for a long while.

Stay with me in the moments when the chest begins to feel the pressure of being called out. Stay with me when you find your brows furrowed as you realize that there is a different perspective of the same situation you deal with day in and day out. Stay with me until the end of this book so you can take away all that I have to say. I am here to remind you that you are not alone. When you begin to wonder if you are balancing life correctly. When you start feeling like you have absolutely nothing, all the while sitting in a place that holds everything you do have, just as a result of comparing your life to a life that is not yours. Or when you want to just give up on what made your heart the most full just because you didn't receive your expected amount of likes. Stay with me. Let me teach you what I have learned. Not through statistics, but through my own experiences and observations. Let me teach you from the lens of my life. Let me help you, comfort you, send love to you through these numbing times, let me educate you. From the bottom.

Now I am not totally ungrateful for this advance in technology, though I feel like the world can easily crumble at any given moment. I am also not resenting the fact that our generation seems to be the one to blame when it comes to the era of Snapchat, Instagram, TikTok, Facebook, etc. Having the spotlight on us as the "generation to look out for" just because we have very tech savvy brains, is a given.

I can admit I didn't feel the finger pointing at us when MySpace was introduced, but at that age I was a teen and I also wasn't aware of the opportunities that really lie within our tablets and computers back then. Now we have many young intelligent individuals creating platforms that generate a buffet full of dopamine flavored desserts that instantly attract any person who has the storage to download the app and try it out. So when it comes to my generation, and being in my thirties, having experienced the beginning of social media, watching new platforms develop continuously, and being able to catch on and grab a hold of these apps by the horns, riding through all these changes in life even when I feel like I am about to fall off and get stomped on; yeah, I can see now how we all might look. It probably looks as though we all agree with these changes simply because we are professionals at adapting to them.

The most adaptable generation has become the generation to blame.

* * * * * * *

There are so many pros to these changes in our world. But those cons, oh boy, oh boy, those cons can begin to really take control. Let us start with a beautiful pro when it comes to social media. Let me take you back to a moment when I really felt the benefits. First example, these apps have connected this vast world together in just one tiny click of a button.

E.F.T.B.

This humongous planet in which we all reside, has become condensed into a world available to anyone without needing a passport, or even currency to get there. If you find wifi, you can fly. I am blessed to be able to stay connected with friends that I felt I had to wish a farewell to, over 4,000 miles across the sea. We spent the last couple of days together saying our goodbyes, giving our last hugs before departing from one another, allowing the Mediterranean Sea to come between our friendship.

The moment when this vast world shrunk down to the click of a button was when I felt the love and presence from this lovely individual. I heard the coin drop alert sound on my phone as it lit up my screen. I began reading a comment from my dear friend on a picture I had posted to Facebook. The comment read, "Safe flight, can't wait to see you again xxx". That notification for me, was the bridge that connected my two worlds together. The world that I was leaving behind in Europe, as I boarded the plane; to the other world where I assumed once I landed back in the states, I would never see my dearest friend until my next trip back. Well my friends, as long as you have wifi, the distance goes from plane rides, layovers, and immigration lines, to clicking open a notification alert and receiving a warm, and virtual hug.

Even with the few benefits of technology and pros that come with these social media options, in my opinion there are just way more poisonous aspects of these habits and the worst part about this is that the poison has already spread through each and every user. When I look around and see the success of these apps, I begin to get angry on the inside because I know when the time comes to blame social media for the symptoms that actually are rooted from all these apps, the finger is going to point right passed instagram, passed facebook, and point right at all of the individuals in the generation I grew up in. It will be our fault that this world is becoming more numb as humans and more intriguing as 2D characters.

I am this generation, therefore I am part of the blame.

* * * * * * *

This book was encouraged after a conversation with a resident at an assisted living home that I used to work at years ago. After our conversation, I held this feeling of blame when he was expressing every opinion he had on the technology in this world today. Oh and you better believe I was listening fully! There was no chance I was going to fall for that coin drop that I heard inside of my coat pocket. If there was ever a moment I was being tested, it was right then and there. I chose to listen to him and give him my undivided attention. Yes I received a notification, it could have been a red notification from instagram on my picture I posted 2 hours ago, it could be a comment on my Facebook wall, oh or it could be a snapchat response to my story that was about to expire from when I was in the gym yesterday working out. Anyways, I didn't dare find out what just alerted my phone and I quickly brushed off the itch that I was feeling just to check.

I was open to all of his thoughts on how the world is now, we organically went back and forth on our thoughts and observations on this unexpected topic that sprouted. I was so invested in every story he told me about his youth and his memories that kept his smile on his face even at such an old age. As his mobility became harder to navigate, his memories within his mind, the stories he spoke, the images in his head that he illustrated through his words were what kept him going at this point. It was a beautiful moment. It was the moment I decided to plant the seed for this book, Education From the Bottom. I hope that this book turns from my planted seed into a continuous spread of beautiful flowers of hope all around this world. I hope this book sits on the shelves and awaits your decision to grab and read and you become motivated to pass this book on like a flower you would pick for that special someone.

In a world full of bitmojis, I hope this book will remind us to put the device down more often than not and smell the flowers.The older generations may have taken lemons and made lemonade, well, you can say for us, we took a filter and we made perfection.

But nothing is ever perfect my friends. Let's begin.

*   *   *   *   *   *   *

It was a really dark day, even though the forecast was sunny with a warm loving breeze, my perspective of the world was cloudy. I decided to put my best self out there and though I strive to put my best self out there everyday, this day I was much more determined. So I put myself together. Makeup, styled the hair, muted the white noise in my mind that was trying so hard to persuade me that these efforts are actually 100% pointless. Then, once I felt absolutely complete and proud of myself for the self care lovin', I decided to open up snapchat. I picked a filter and captured a smile and I hit story. As I opened the bathroom door to begin my day all of my followers would be clicking through and passing by my still photo of my face; lips puckered, eyes slightly squinting with a touch of seduction, and my aura screaming "Im confident!". What they saw was myself ready to conquer the day, and that I did. Until the moment right before bed when I revisited that same mirror in the bathroom for one last look. Right when I assumed victory was mine, I was slapped in the face by reality when I saw my reflection looking back at my unfiltered me.

Instead of being sad about who I really was I decided to prove myself wrong and I challenged myself in that moment to post a selfie without any filter just to make a statement with myself. So I lifted my chin up just a bit, and my arm higher, and I clicked the button for a selfie. Just as it does in a scary movie, right as the scene begins to get more intense, the sound effects become more shaper and more loud, those were the vibes I was feeling. I felt like I was in a scary movie where the confident woman was never really there. I couldn't find her. I failed to find her and capture that proud beautiful woman from this morning all because I didn't have the help from a filter. This filter had trimmed down my nose a tad, enhanced my color with a bit of bronzer to my face, plumped up my lips just a bit, and curved my eye shape too. Without a filter, I felt like I was not enough. Without a filter I was not even able to make the cut when trying out for a lead in my own damn story. I couldn't make myself proud enough. I couldn't bear to see my face in my own phone, never mind allow my followers to stare into my embarrassment.

"You" I said to myself as I peered through the tears that flooded my eyes and I focused on the woman in the mirror. It was my own finger pointing at my reflection that day. I put the blame on myself for having allowed and accepted filters to become a part of my confidence. Without them I was not good enough. It is hard. Hard to just be. To just, watch. To just entertain our minds with past memories. It's hard to just listen. To love, to hide, to live. With all these ever growing features and updates that we feel obligated to adapt too and download it only seems like the problem is becoming more complex. As the apps improve, the difficulty to just "be" increases. Since forever our human instinct is to keep improving. To be better than before. How can one really be mad at the successful person who created these platforms? As they continue to improve features all I want to do is improve myself. The irony in this is I find myself pressing download on the software update instead of choosing to concentrate on myself and update my own being. I chose 100% to not be angry with the creators of all these platforms. But I want to be absolutely clear that as their passion to increase the success of technology flames up and excels, it is burning our souls with it.

If you choose to be bitter about the changes in life, you're just going to become miserable. Every single day all things around us are continuously changing, including ourselves. We need to put more time into understanding the importance of our own personal growth. Once we reprioritize ourselves and realize the importance of our own growth, the bitterness we may feel as the virtual world expands will slowly but surely become non-existent. That's just the thing. We will learn that though we can't change the technology advances around us, we can change how we react to it. We can change how much time we give to it. We can change how much importance it holds to us as individuals. We need to first remind ourselves of the importance of change, for our own sake. Someone who sits around each day just to witness the updates in our virtual reality and continues to overwhelm themselves with the extreme power that these apps have over the world, could eventually become a bitter human.

It is fascinating how much these devices can influence our minds, bodies and our souls. Have you felt busy lately just as a side effect of your efforts to change yourself and add value to your life? I encourage you to stay busy with improving who you are as a person. This way you personally have something else to watch and monitor, other than the posts, stories, and pictures that scroll through the phone. Instead you can watch your own personal growth. You can work on the updates that have to do with pushing towards a better you.

Let's ease off on the habit of searching for validation from our followers. I have used this bit of awareness within my own life and I can say that yes, I am beginning to be proud of the reflection in the mirror all over again.

CHAPTER 2

CLEAN UP THE MESS
DON'T AVOID THE MESS

I can only imagine what my grades would be like if I had this lifestyle as a student in middle school, high school, college, wherever you choose to sit and expand your knowledge. With the extremity of the phone, I wouldn't put it passed the school systems to sooner or later create a symbol in the shape of an iPhone that would illustrate a grade that means: Well we don't know if you are lacking learning capabilities for this subject or if you're just interested in your phone more than the lesson. It is all so toxic, but we have figured out a way to live with it and accept it all. Therefore we built immunity for this toxic way of life. Some days I am on edge and emotional with the differences that we face from back then until now. Years ago I almost caught myself crying as my son played with mud and sticks. Were the tears forming from my disappointment of his new Jordan sneakers being fully disrespected by the mud? Or were the tears forming because it was clear that he still held the innocence of his mind and still had a vibrant imagination without the influences of the world around him? It was such a beautiful moment. I can see the tablets and this new "way of life" knocking at his door each day. When the mornings become a bit rough I see myself throwing the cartoons on, or letting him have his time in front of the iPad with kids YouTube on. This moment with the mud and sticks was more than just crying about the dirt we were about to bring into the house, but it was the slither of chance I was witnessing. The slither of chance I was holding onto.

Being a parent can be exhausting and very tedious. There will be so many moments when we want to just solve the problem of pure exhaustion and let the virtual vibrant colors babysit our children. I have surrendered so many times when I wanted to bring the kids outside to the park but my fatigue had a much better idea and allow them to have extra screen time so I can get a mental break. I get it, it can be tough and I am not bashing your decisions one bit! I see the world that we are in today and no, I am not going to put shame on any person's way of parenting. One thing I have learned as a mother is I do not do all things right, but I do my best. If I had a random stranger tell me this it may come off as an insult, if I have it in myself to remind myself that I am doing alright and the best I can, then there is no need to search for further validation. Don't get me wrong either, Youtube for the kids has so many benefits. When I first began writing out this book, it was about 7 years ago which means my daughter had not entered the chat yet (kidding), but it was when I just had my son.

I was so thankful for Youtube for the moments when I needed to really take a second for myself without the worry of him getting into the wrong things. I would watch my son watch YouTube and videos of little kids playing in mud, splashing the camera lens with muddy water, laughing and running, not waiting when the adult in the video giggled and trailed them yelling "wait!". I would watch him crack a small smile in front of a screen that displayed a child his age running energetically around, getting messy, testing the limits, learning, and playing. This also brings me back to why when I witnessed my son playing with dirt and rocks, it was more than just an emotional mom moment. But I was proud of myself for just letting go of rules and the perfect cut out ideas we create and fantasize about as parents and instead of him staying clean and watching another kid live their life via YouTube, I just let go of all expectations and let him get his shoes muddy, and let his smile shine. Youtube or go outside? Watch kids get dirty in video while kids stay clean and watch on an iPad? Go outside and have a ball and worry about the clean up when the time comes or distract them with reels? I can go on and on with questions like these. This would be a good time to ask yourself these same choices and just out of curiosity see which way you decide to go. The best way to initiate change is to admit that something is in need of change.

So yes, I most definitely became sensitive when I saw my son playing with those rocks and mud that day. When I watched him pick up a stick and create the most medieval sword in his mind to keep away the bad guys, I could not help but adore the simplicity. Another part of me will become sensitive but in a more negative light, when I bring up the moment when I witnessed my daughter enhance her crawl at turbo speed when I place my cellphone on the ground in hope to bribe her to reach that distance. I was positioned right behind the phone but even with the repetitive calling of her name and making silly faces, her motivation was at a bare minimum. It was the moment I placed my phone on the ground and stopped recording to continue with the faces and shouting her name that I realized she picked up momentum. I always wondered if she felt the urge to crawl because she could actually see mama's face or if it was once the phone was placed down that this little device had the power to motivate my baby enough to encourage her to crawl.

Kaitlyn Thompson

* * * * * * *

The idea of kids and social media is an active study that we are all currently a part of. Parent or not, we are all a part of this experiment. It is the years now where we are producing information that will one day support a researcher's conclusion on the influences that social media has placed on our beautiful world. I can go on and on about children and the connection with social media. I could go on a rant about how it was as a new mom and the power I felt when I chose not to upload my son's face to the internet right away. I can go on and on and explain why I felt more powerful uploading my daughter's face while still in the hospital because I felt more confident that social media was nowhere as powerful as this feeling of being a mother of two. I could go on and tell you about the time when I stood behind my son and watched him as he experimented with bitmoji characteristics while he built his avatar for the 2D reality. I remember sitting there and looking at my perfect handsome son, watching him try his best to create this vision for himself that his 2D reality would accept, and admire. I can literally continue on topics relating to parenthood, the funny, the desperate, the sad, the astonishing, but that is for another time, and another book.

It's humorous because we continuously have updates on our devices of different platforms showing us a new way of navigating through them. The new features, and the exciting new emojis. We used to believe we were watching our phone update but in reality, the device is watching the way we adapt. We have become the product and it is time to reclaim the true importance of emotions. We need to take the power back of doing, of living, of moving, and of simply being. It is time to realize and congratulate the successes of each multimillionaire as we clearly witness their product become a top hit! It's a proud moment, and yes it is an amazing moment to be able to have this accessible to us, all the time. We can lay in bed and watch a beautiful cuisine being constructed in the depths of the mountains while the chef creates heat under a rock and butter begins to sizzle on the rocks of Mother Earth. We can stroke our best friends' egos and slide down their feed and comment on every post they have and remind them that you are here for the hype and the love forever and always. You can be in a living room full of your immediate family and not say one thing out loud but can laugh at a meme sent in a group message via instagram because it brings you all back to those childhood days.

As I bring up all these examples I am not here to call us out or make us feel bad. I don't want to make us feel that we have done wrong up to this point. I am just saying to you that the sky is blue, and the grass is green, water is an essential to living, and our phones should be forgotten purposely for a couple of hours each day.

Let it ring when someone needs your attention. If someone needs your attention, they will find you. Ever think of that? If someone needs to get a hold of you, if they are in dire need, they will figure it out. Now if there is a system in motion with you and lets say a family member and the phone is a crucial part in staying alert to one's health and wellbeing, then please take my advice lightly and understand that I am not saying let them down, but I am trying to share a different perspective on a topic we all personally feel genius on.

* * * * * * *

Let us not continue giving these devices so much power, and let's begin to pull it back just a little. Let us fall back in love with telling our stories more and really bringing the listener into the moment that you are explaining, because this way that story will stay with them forever, rather than the risk of being tapped through or worse, allowing your story to not having access to viewing it, after 24 hours of it being posted.

CHAPTER 3

VIDEOS FOR LONGEVITY NOT JUST, 24 HOURS

Wow, to think back to those camcorder days! Having the choice to pop in an old video of myself as a child, running towards the camera with my shirt falling off one shoulder and a large smile on my face with just one goal in mind, to take up the whole camera screen with my face. My desire to attract all the attention. Aspiring to make a movie that would want to be played over and over again. A homemade video that would bring the family together in front of the tv and I could witness their reactions to a video that I created! Oh the fun that used to be. This choice unfortunately is not available to my kids anymore. For example my kids have millions of short clips throughout my phone, Tik Toks, reel attempts, they even have videos in my camera roll that say "Hey guys today on this episode" just to mimic what they have learned from having a relationship with technology. It's just that nostalgia that is felt when you come across a picture or see a camcorder hanging out on someone's shelf nowadays. That feeling of setting up a family camcorder, pressing record, running back into the frame and just going for it; then to plugging it into the tv to play it back and watch what we have created. Well this process not only took creativity but it took time. Now we have Tik Toks that require little to no creativity, and it can be uploaded in the matter of 60 seconds. There's no need for effort in many categories of life. But that is really what makes life all worthwhile! The effort to make the memories, and now we are becoming accustomed to memories that take no effort therefore mean less and life is slowly becoming meaningless as well. Dramatic? Well clearly, that's what I am here for.

Because of the convenience of phone videos, it has just become the new norm to omit our previous devices. While I have your attention on issues like this one I am going to drop in a bit of advice if you're an owner of technology devices similar to camcorders, drone cameras, voice recorders, and devices similar to these. I do highly suggest investing in a storage bin that can keep cords and chargers away from water damage or any other kind of damage just so you have access to the devices that you put your trust, money, and precious memories into. Even to this day, knowing the camcorder sits in a closet without the proper attachment to charge it up and the difficulty it is to find a store that carries this particular charger it really has been the only reason I haven't been able to press play on my young self as I take up the whole tv screen with my shirt sliding off my shoulder and my young imagination soaring.

And it's those moments after when you pick up your phone to search for nearest store with a camcorder charger and then the internet leads you to many other multiverses within the social media universe and next thing you know your watching reels on how to use an at home green screen and camcorder to make a real life action thriller movie.

I mean the examples could go on and on. Even when we are consciously trying to steer away from a toxic habit, there will always be another option that is going to test your willpower and remind you that the toxic choice is still available! Social Media can be so tempting!

Please don't get me wrong either, the quick access to using the phone and recording is absolutely amazing and the convenience of this in our fast paced world goes hand in hand, but the videos and the memories they just don't promise longevity. Yes your archives can go on and on for years and years, but will your kids or your kids' kids be able to get access to your phone, know your password, to get into your archives and really get to a moment that they were longing for? Just to reminisce. I record videos that are so precious in my phone and getting them deleted to make storage or accidentally pressing trash are just a couple of ways to demonstrate the common way to lose precious memories.

It tests your values when you find yourself watching uh I don't know,   a pig race at the fair.

You're really feeling this urge to just record it.

Why, though?

Well, Who cares.

But the storage is full.

So you go through to your videos and delete little icons that hold 2+   minutes of probably a beautifully captured moment but in order to get   this footage, and the easy access to press delete and take the power of   precious memories away, we fix the problem quickly and with such   determination. Delete.

Trash.

Now we have space for a pig race.

So yes this is a downfall to videos recorded conveniently. Another not so positive feeling is what we get when we witness someone who is walking around with a camcorder to capture home videos. We automatically gain this alertness that this person has a goal to capture a moment forever. Nowadays we don't even know if someone is checking the weather or recording you into their personal files when their phone is positioned in your direction. So therefore we have lost the difference to notice the value of a moment by witnessing it being captured on a video camera for longevity or if it's just being recorded on a story for 24 hours and then eventually vanishing into the attic of archives.

* * * * * * *

I don't want to admit the amount of videos I have stored of my kids on my phone because more than half of them are tampered with by a filter. My children are perfect. Absolutely perfect. But I find myself swiping left and I swipe left until I find a filter that makes my mind say "approved". Approved of what!? My kids have my approval, without any goddamn filter so what in the world would I be approving? Who am I really aiming to impress? Is it that I am trying to impress a certain person or group? Is it shameful just because I love to see this filter over everyone in my pictures? Is it because I am protecting my kids' raw image from this virtual reality? Just by writing these thoughts down and admitting this moment to you all I am realizing is the need for more natural raw footage of my children. The ratio of natural to filtered is not fair and not appreciated. I want to forever appreciate the curves, the lines, the temporary scrapes, the milk mustaches of my children. Now that I am aware of these habits I will make sure to capture the moments that mean the most with no filters added. I will use the convenience of the phone to make home videos but I will not fall into that old habit of filtering just to impress the eyes via social media platforms. I am ruining footage that later on in life will be more precious if it is more authentic. The dog nose and licking tongue? Super cute, but it's my young child that I am in search of, not the trending filters during that time.

Fads go in and out of style but the memories of our personal youth and the young ones around us, those moments will never go out of style. Building awareness on this little yet powerful fact in a world like today is all that we can do. We are the generation that has yet to be in control, we continuously have variables changing all around us and we can only make the best out of the situations we are handed. Most of the time we may not even agree with these changes but if we don't adapt and hold on, we feel like we fell off. With all of this "power" that we seem to hold, you would think this generation would eventually feel in charge of our own lives.

Maybe it starts with just speaking out loud about the way we feel instead of typing it into a numb virtual world. The generation of genius minds, and creative innovators, the ones to point the finger at because we have created this monster, and yet we still can't seem to tame the beast. A good venting session on a Facebook status may help ease our frustration. I say do it! It's not only fun, it relieves a little of the pressure that we have when we hold onto a feeling and keep it bottled up inside. But do not get confused with distributing the pressure and eliminating the pressure. Posting about it will help distribute the pain you have from one platform in your 2D life to the other platform, but it will still be with you until you let those emotions flow and once you actually talk through them. Do not just post about it, speak about it. Be about it.

*   *   *   *   *   *   *

We vent online about some issues that really have a toll on us. We go back a week from that moment feeling like a whole new person and we come across that post when we were in such a dark place. We see the 28 Likes, the 4 Comments, and we are brought right back to that moment we thought we let go of. We catch a glimpse of a moment where we felt most vulnerable. Though we saw through it and feel much better since this time, we are able to see the process of how we dealt with it, we either see the abundance of support that we got when we wrote this post, or we see the weak amounts of support. Why are we allowing the pain that we felt previously and then overcame, to come back in full vengeance all because it will have the power to sit on your timeline forever and ever, awaiting you to just scroll by so it can remind you that even though you came far, your past will always be a part of you until you realize the power in letting it go.

If it no longer serves you, why are you still holding onto that moment? Vulnerable posts where we seek support from our followers reap rewards and then will turn around and pull you back down into that dark place all over again. Because in this 2D world, you can be great, and you can be "not great" and then you can be great again. It's in our real world, where we can be great, feel like shit, dive into our feelings and find out what is hurting us, grow from it, learn from it, evolve, and 360 into a better version of ourselves.

CHAPTER 4

ALL MOUTH NO EAR

If there is a mic that is unoccupied, it is bound to be used. The same goes for every media outlet. The problem with these platforms is the audience. The ones who are watching you speak are not just sitting and listening. They are actually sitting and waiting for their turn to speak. There is a difference in the quietness of an auditorium full of people listening and absorbing versus an auditorium full of people who are sitting there thinking about what they are going to say when you finish your thought. So first step to speaking awareness into a crowd full of people who can be either of the two, you will need to find the right microphone. You can't just assume that every microphone that is abandoned is the one that will project your voice out in an inspirational way. Some microphones will be found deep within a post battle on Facebook. This microphone will look a lot like a comment box and you will pick up the microphone and you will speak your mind fully and proud. But don't you see? You read the post and you made sure to speak. I know it seems like I am trying to encourage people to not have functioning conversations but I am not saying that one bit. There just comes a time and a place for feedback. Nowadays, Facebook encourages feedback and yes that's great. But it can be harmful. Not only will you be pushing your own morals or values on someone else's post but you have created my theory to be true by just commenting back to someone's opinion. Let others use the microphone and listen to what they say. Let it sink in. Do some personal work.

Do you agree?

Do you disagree?

Do you want to see content like this on your timeline?

Do you feel you just want to comment "Your NUTS!"?

Do you really hear them?

Or are you just waiting to talk?

So when you come across that "abandoned mic" ask yourself, is this the stage where I want to perform? Is the audience going to listen to me or do they want to use the microphone right after? I feel that this small detail (when compared to the grand scheme of things) is very important, because when it comes to finding the right place to speak and express, I think, I found mine. This book. This decision to create a place to put down all of my thoughts and lead you on a journey that takes you through my mind and through all of my experiences. This book hopes to prove to you that we actually aren't alone in some of the tough moments that we live through. And then I find myself even wondering, will the readers actually stay with me as I speak through these chapters? Are you really listening? Or are you the percentage that is already brainstorming a response to this? Will people feel sympathetic to my failing attempt to change the world? Or will this attempt be viewed as a success considering it is in the hands of yourself? All of these questions seem to always destroy that silent calmness in my mind. My insecurities always scream, and my doubts ramble on and on like a child during the peak of their sugar rush. I know I am not going to stop our addiction to SnapChat videos or writing our raw emotions into a status. I am not here for that. It is your life, and we can never forget that we have the ability to do what we please with our own.

It is definitely in my opinion sad at times to see how life is turning out (and the rapid speed of destruction at that) but I am not one to sit back and judge everything that is occurring around me. If someone is SnapChatting their meals and choosing to hold onto their starvation just a second longer just to show their followers what they are about to dive into, that's cool. Or if someone is choosing to give their attention to their phone and not their crying kid that is disrupting the whole cafe, well that unfortunately is a choice that was made as well. The goal to get your undivided attention was not so I could express how much I disapprove of this or how I would never do that, because I for sure did not create a book to make an outlet for me to talk down on anyone or any situation. I do feel it is my place to say it's time to build awareness on the way we react to the world around us. As you read this book right now, what is happening around you? What are you tolerating? Are you tuning something out to stay focused with me?

* * * * * * *

It is time in all aspects of our lives to rebuild our awareness in every aspect of our daily routines. It is time we begin to fully live our lives again instead of only showing our lives. I feel like when I first thought to create this book it went from a simple topic that I knew I could stay fully engaged with, but over the years it has grown a little more intense and therefore what is said within these pages are said with a little bit more base in my voice. I am getting serious! Don't get me wrong though, as serious as I am on this topic, my tone is still completely chill. My finger is not pointing at you because our virtual world is affecting us negatively, my finger is pointing at you because I choose you to be the start of a really, really necessary change.

Pointing fingers at us and making us feel like the villains all because we choose to make the best of our today has begun to make us dread our tomorrows. We need to just stop being angry at one another for going with the flow of this ever-changing world and instead we need to give ourselves a little boost on the priority scale. I feel we should start to focus on enhancing our mental state along with the world's advances. We need to make sure to update our minds at the same speed that we are receiving those software updates that seem to knock on our door until we decide to answer.

Speaking of those software updates, they usually take around like 10 or 15 minutes for the update to be complete. What do we do when our phone is busy at work fixing its software so all the technology in the world strives to stay up to speed with one another? What do you decide to do with these minutes? Did you say 'this seems like a perfect time to meditate'? Did you say during these precious minutes I will focus on my breathing and set intentions for myself when I am not using my phone? Or did we just distract yourself in such a pointless way to make the time go by so you could disguise your excitement of seeing the new updates and finding out what new emojis and 2D emotions we are granted and offered to use and feel? We were born into this world of uniqueness and truth and then we signed ourselves up for a virtual world full of rules, characters and filtered lies. This is your life. In the end, no matter if it's reality or virtual or both combined, if you are really and authentically happy, then I am extremely happy for you and your happiness. Enjoying it is all I ask, however that may be! I am just here, speaking to you to say,

Hey you, what you felt that day, while laying in bed feeling as though   the day already won, all those feelings? Those were real feelings. And   those feelings are okay to be felt. Sit with them and don't be afraid to   feel them. You may start to feel trapped in your physical body because   you feel that you aren't allowed to express these vulnerable states   online because that behavior is not allowed. Because that behavior   won't receive likes and that's all that life has come too. If it won't   receive the Likes, we believe that we aren't Liked either. If you need to hear it, I love you. You may feel alone but you are with me, as with everyone else and we are all just trying. Some try with a filter, others try by avoiding the 2D world all together. If you feel knocked down, if you feel like gravity is too heavy in this 3 dimensional world, and you would rather live through your phone and keep your beautiful self locked in a room on this earth, that's okay. I don't agree with you, but That's okay. Sometimes we need a day, or two. But don't waste your   life believing that you are alone and have lost hope in the person you see when you look in your reflection. Don't forget about that double tap in your chest that is continuously beating. It is beating not because it Likes you but because it Loves you.

CHAPTER 5

THE WORLD IS FLAT

Soaring over the ripples of a still ocean, flying high over the bristles of the trees that make up a rainforest, swooping low over the dry concrete paths of the tropic islands, feeling the sun change from warmth, to extreme heat, to just a source of light. Watching the rivers make their way downhill finding one slope to another, until it finds a place where it belongs. This world, this huge, amazing and beautiful world has finally come together. All sorts of places and all types of people, all different routines yet we share the same common meeting place. The virtual world. All of these apps, and the social media platforms have created a virtual universe where distance is no longer an issue. This universe allows us to screenshot an opinion, like peoples faces, change our features into a 'doggy', make our own flaws vanish into mid air, where there is no more catfish per se, but instead it has become how do you say it #hashtag shark week.

Those small innocent alterations become too overwhelming that the lies we created start to become the forced truth. For example you can't post a selfie to instagram with your pimple removed and then make an appearance on snapchat with a huge disgusting zit. So you take that innocent alteration and filter it on all other platforms because well… we don't want to be a liar now do we? We no longer know what is real and what is not. I know it may seem dramatic when I drop a line like this but if someone is going to get all deep into this type of conversation, just to simply have a conversation about it, why sugar coat it? One thing about apps and platforms and everything in this cyber world, is that we can hurt feelings. It's okay if I admit that we are losing sight of what is real and what is not, and it's okay if I say it one thousand times in a row. One thing to realize about Instagram, Twitter, Tik Tok, Facebook, every neighborhood of the virtual world, is that they will never get mad at you for taking time away from using the app, and they won't send you a message saying "hey we are angry because you expressed the negative influence our app has on your life. It doesn't even support itself enough to be concerned about our well being! These applications are solely interested in the benefits they will receive, it doesn't give a crap if they are benefitting us individually. Yes there are ads that will advertise ways to stay healthy and how to stay motivated using this or taking that, but that's just another crumb to the bigger trap. They don't really care, they are just trying to keep you online. They just want to keep you scrolling. This is something to really think about. These apps are not the products. We are the products, because they would be useless without our desire to use them.

* * * * * * *

E.F.T.B.

We no longer know what is real and what is not. We even become confused with the attention we receive and begin making ourselves believe its love instead of simply a "Like". Let's even consider the thought of any individual eager to find a date or a potential companion. The trouble we face with finding love in this virtual mess is the challenge to differentiate our double tap on a picture from a simple notification of interest. Ah! Maybe a message? A private DM? Sadly this choice in action has morphed into more of a "slutty route" rather than simply showing interest in one another. From all the rap songs that express sliding into a dm, now it is becoming so hard to simply view it as a sign of admiration. To live and to love should be completely effortless! But with this day and age and all the complications we have to deal with we just learn to tough it out and find out how to make do with the fact that finding love just isn't a priority in the 2D cyber world. We have learned to just listen to our parents' love stories because theirs, well, theirs didn't expire after 24 hours of viewing.

* * * * * * *

It is so hard to bring back a trend that seems so out of reach. I say this because what I see online when in connection with love is a lot of failed attempts. I see many trials with love, and instead of it being viewed as an error if things go wrong, we are starting to view it as the "wrong swipe". The trend that I am speaking about is falling in love, finding your person, getting married! It just doesn't seem to be the trend that is going viral and therefore the desire to reach the goal of finding your person has dropped very low on the importance ladder.

I just recently married my best friend (shout out to my handsome, Kwame Thompson) and it is really such a magical feeling. I feel powerful not because my identity is paired with his now, but because, I feel like I accomplished something for myself. I proved to myself that love can be effortless, that the love stories that seem like the Grease musical, or the Titanic, can be completely real. Through all the dating apps that have surfaced while being in a relationship with my husband, I can personally say I have never had an account nor needed to use this app in search of love. I have a very very light perspective on this topic because I was never a user of this. When I do hear stories that come from Tinder dates and Bumble conversations I always found myself wondering what standards and criteria did these applicants need to hold in order to qualify for a date. The moment I first ever met my husband, back in college, I always say and I know I will never forget, was that zap of chemistry that radiated from my vision to his. I felt this whole area of space around his body that was reserved for me. I could see the space that was waiting for me to just close in and seal the deal. I felt it and I wonder if the ones who use dating apps can feel this type of chemistry through the apps as well? I am a strong believer in love. Finding it is always the best part of the story. I only wish that when love is found through an app that the search for chemistry isn't just out the window. If you feel a good vibe with your bitmojis or behind the screens of your phone but in person you can just see that "this isn't it" then don't settle. Also if you keep getting fooled with the app and this outcome occurs more often than not, then take the old approach and go out on the town, take your face out of your phone and look around to see what the universe decided to send to you. You never know, maybe your potential partner is reading this book right now too and later today with the motivation I just sent to you, tonight may be the night you find one another.

It really does all work out in the end. This phrase is a phrase that only works when you're at a point that is becoming beneficial to you. What I am trying to say is when we are in the thick of something and life seems really hard to handle and someone walks in and drops this line "It really does all work out in the end" that seems kind of belittling to the emotions we are dealing with. But if we take this phrase and really deconstruct it we begin to assume it can't be the absolute end then because not one thing is working in our favor. When it comes to my perspective, and this phrase. I can relate. I am in my thirties and I started the first draft of this imaginary book in my mid twenties. I am so proud that I had this vision at this age, because having started this book then has created a long range of time and experiences that I can truly express within these pages. I am over the moon proud of myself for not looking at this unfinished project as a failure and actually seeing that it hadn't quite worked out completely yet, because maybe it wasn't quite the end. So here I am, and yes this phrase works at this moment for myself. I really needed those extra years in between to really make this book hold the weight that it does.

We can all read a book, full of words, words with heavy meaning and once we finish there is absolutely no meaning to the book at all. Those are scary moments when we realize that we put trust in the front page and put our faith in the idea that there would be some sort of intriguing or meaningful relatable lesson in the midst of those pages. Just to find out that we have been fooled. I think If I were to have jumped on this concept in my mid twenties and rushed the process then I wouldn't have been able to do the "work". What's the work? By this I mean, made an Instagram account. By this I mean, learn how to work the Instagram reels. Figure out how to create a proper bitmoji that didn't make it obvious that I wish I had a different structure of a chin. Learn the proper way to grab the attention of all my friends on Facebook. Find out the pressure of actually "going live" on any social media platform. Learn the eight counts to a dance and repeat the moves till I was post worthy on Tik Tok. By this I mean to discover the world of archives and find the powerful feeling of archiving 400 of my posts and only having 4 special moments in my life for people to dive into. I wouldn't have been able to watch myself evolve from being a "filtering mother", to a "post the raw footage or no post at all", mother. I mean there are so many years in between this book that I didn't realize I actually needed. If my main message from this novel is just to express the pressure and the overwhelming effects that social media can have on an individual and how to control the amount of pressure that is applied, then it was extremely mandatory that I had those years in between so I could do my research. I know what you're all thinking, this chick really is saying research when in reality she is opening up her Instagram and clicking through everyones stories. Well, maybe I am a smarter chick than you may think because I took an everyday moment, one that comes freely to us, and I turned it into a potentially big influence to all of humanity.

* * * * * * *

E.F.T.B.

Let's get back to that going Live topic for a second too. It is such a strange and funny concept to realize. Not only is there a button that gives the option of going live on the feed but it is not as popular as you would have imagined it to be. It is like an experiment and the outcome supported the predictions. It's funny sometimes seeing one of our users "Going Live" and thinking twice about accepting it and then coming to realize we avoid going into their live chat room because we feel our 2D mask is being slightly tugged on. It is the closest to humanity. Going live on any social media platform is the closest to humanity and you can see that the ones who are famous will get millions of viewers to check into their live, and the friends from high school with the perfect post and abundance of likes still have a room full of 20 viewers who are able to ignore the pressure of accepting the live invitation and walk their username into the live video. If you felt a bit of heat on the top of your ears then you really related to what I just said. If you felt a little relief from the front of your brain after reading that then you were just proved that when you did avoid the live it was probably for the same reasons and it feels a bit amazing knowing you're not strange for avoiding a live, you're just aware of the powers of 2D and didn't want to strip any of that away.

Not only has the virtual world become more and more complex, but it is an illusion of what is real. This illusion is so properly thought out that it gives us the tiniest taste of truth. We begin to crave the desire to express ourselves all the time through our phones and tablets that we begin overindulging in this version of what's true and eventually we realize we have been binge eating on false hope.

As a matter of fact, we are not overindulging, we are in starvation mode. We have been craving human connection, genuine relationships, support, and love from each person we cross paths with for some time now.

For a while it has seemed as though we have found just that, but it's time to take advantage of our time here together, in this world and not just through the web.

*   *   *   *   *   *   *

The power of our usernames.

It all started from viewing one person's story. I could have caught it right in its last hour or I could have viewed it 8m since it's been uploaded, either way I was added to the list of watchers. It's a power. The eye symbol beside my name started to be my power. If I wasn't fond of someone I would try my best to avoid their story because I wanted to make my power feel more superior. I would avoid double tapping pictures to show them that I did NOT like their face on my feed. I would avoid reading into their captions because I didn't want to know what they were trying to tell me. Why do we not have the option to dislike an instagram post? Why are there options to report a comment or a post? It all seems like instagram actually does care about our feelings when in reality at the end of the day it is creating monsters out of the most perfect people. What makes us think that taking our tag name away from the action will illustrate clearly that we are angry or frustrated?

I have learned throughout my research and experiences with social media, that the timeline starts to become like your "circle of friends". Let me just dive into this concept quickly. What I am trying to say is we often hear that you are who your friends are. It does make sense, if your friends are a group of spontaneous free birds, you'll most likely go on more trips and adventures than the friend group who would hang out in the commons on a blanket with smoothies and books. So when it comes to your timeline and you see posts on cooking tutorials, scroll after scroll, you'll most likely want to get creative in the kitchen. If you see a lot of followers wearing little to no clothes scroll after scroll after scroll, you'll most likely want to experiment sooner or later and see what kind of attention you can attract just by doing what your timeline is doing. Who are you surrounding yourself with? This brings me back to when I was expressing my desire for an UnLike button, and then I realized, I have control over who I am around. Deleting, removing, unfriending, decluttering, it has become an active ongoing movement for myself in the virtual world. Once you friend someone they don't have to be permanently there. If it doesn't make you feel good to see a certain post, why surround yourself with anything that encourages your smile to fade? If you needed the green light to go and purge your friends list, well then here it is.

On your mark, get set, green light.

We are being stripped away of our feelings. We go into this app where we are only allowed to stroke the egos of others. We log into an application where egos are welcome but please leave your vulnerability at the door. I can actually visualize some instagram tags of people who don't leave their vulnerability at the door and I praise them right now. Right here in this moment, in this sentence I want you to know that maybe you did not receive an abundance of likes on a the post where you expressed how much you miss a loved one, but I am glad that you made a subconscious deal with yourself that it's not about to feedback with this one. You wanted to get it off your chest. It's just simply not about the feedback. This world is turning us into validation whores. Why do we feel we need to be validated for the things that make us happy?

I could post a picture of my favorite pot in my clean but not glamorous kitchen. I could take a picture of this pot because this picture would hold a scent in it that makes me feel genuinely so happy and full. It makes me feel comforted and loved, and makes me feel not so alone. It makes me feel this fuzzy warm feeling inside myself, knowing that my kids are upstairs playing just like I used to do when I would sit and play with my toys in a house just like the one that this pot is in. But it's what's in that pot that makes this picture so fulfilling. It is the slices of apples, lemons, and oranges, the cinnamon sticks, the dash of vanilla extract, the star anise herbs floating throughout. That rolling boil that pushes these scents from the water and into the air, filling up my nostrils and flowing through my body bringing me to the most blissful state imagined. It is the picture that held this scent of pure bliss, but to the world- its just a picture of a pot. How many likes would I receive on a picture of the pot on my stovetop? How many people would relate to this warm smell that brings us absolute joy? Those numbers will not match. If we determined the things we loved and admired just through the notifications we received from these platforms, we would lose the very most important things in life that we love most and hold dear to us. I could never put this picture of the pot that brings me joy on my timeline because I know already it won't get the feedback that it deserves. But this is what makes me extremely happy, yet the criteria for a likable post on instagram is an unwritten law in our 2D world rulebook that most of the time we don't even realize we are obeying.

It is also in those years in between, from deciding this book needed to be written and the years up until now that I was able to watch other apps rise from the depths of nowhere. TikTok for example, just coming up from the ashes. You thought instagram and Facebook would be sitting alone in a room forever? Well, knock knock, here's TikToK. It influenced so many users in such a small amount of time and it also influenced the other platforms. This was the beginning of instagram reels, and YouTube reels as well. TikTok is definitely a big contributor to young children and their attention span. It is always hard to keep a child engaged in any activity, I mean they are young and curious and they are nonstop. They have the energy to move from one thing to another to another. This is also the same with Tok Tok. The videos range from watching soda cans being crushed from under a truck's tires (for a satisfying sound effect) to watching a recipe in fast motion of a delicious dessert. The topics on TikTok can go from a sad topic to a silly topic to a trending topic. Just throw the viewers thumbs on a roller coaster seat, buckle them in, check to make sure the thumbs can scroll and can do so comfortably, and then you're off. Building our emotions up and flinging them down, as we get stuck in this tunnel of videos that can only go up to a minute long but yet are so intriguing that you need to watch that one till the end and check out the next because of course it can only get better and better.

I have this voice in my head that says

"Alright that's enough, honestly"

"I think your kids are getting bored"

"One more scroll, just one more scroll"

"Ten more scrolls"

"I should really probably wake up to the world around me already"

That voice does come in occasionally to try and help me to make the wise choice and get off this emotional rollercoaster of wasted minutes but I've learned to welcome the voice sooner and more frequently. This was a big change for myself. I am able to manage my time by listening to that voice right away instead of pushing it off.

But as I've said before I have not done any studies except the ones that I experience on my own, but I can truly say that when I am telling my kids a story I know that if I don't make it interesting and up beat then I will lose their focus. Maybe that is all children, or maybe it's the influence of reels that have encouraged them to learn that if it doesn't grab their attention they can just swipe on by. I find myself many times wondering when the last time was that my kids were actually really and truly devastatingly bored. When was the last time that I actually began to feel bad that my children were so bored in a place that I told myself I would bring them straight to the park after whatever situation we were dealing with was over? I just don't have any memory of this. That is terrifying. I mean it's nice to know that if I was to go to an appointment that was tedious, I know my kids will be okay as they sit on their phones or iPads, but when I really had a moment to think of the last time my kids were actually devastatingly bored, I couldn't think back to it. Is this a good realization, or am I avoiding the best method of teaching obedience?

* * * * * * *

It is also within boredom that we learn the depths of our own brain. It is with boredom that we become vulnerable with our mind and realize what we would rather be doing in that moment. It is with boredom that we create discipline and learn obedience.

It's as if our minds were increasing at such a high rate that someone was given a task to dumb us all down, and it sure looks like they are succeeding with grace. It's as if we were in the position of an absolute breakthrough that we had to get pushed back 100 steps just so we would never reach our fullest potential. I mean once we reach the highest of the highest, what's after that? Well if we never know we will always just wish to get there. Maybe the only way to the highest of our potential is to go back 100 steps first.

We have been stripped into a 2D human, where emotions are limited to the amount of choices we have to click, where we are encouraged to show our successes and whisper bully words into keeping our truest selves locked away in the personal photo albums we keep in our phones. It is truly sad to realize that we were almost there. We were almost in a place where someone would walk up to another person and say wow I like you and I would love to start a conversation with you in hopes to invite you to my home for dinner where I can feed you dishes that are traditional within my culture. We were steps away from sitting at the beach and insisting someone come and join us on your towel and talk about the weekend that we just experienced. We were so close to breaking through this era of racial conflicts, of gender conflicts, conflicts regarding the "American Dream" (so to say) and realizing that life doesn't need to be lived the right way, but the happy way.

Instead we were pushed back so far and stripped away from these feelings and now here we are, faced with new challenges, numb emotions, and completely lost in a world where all our answers are at the tips of our fingers.

Kaitlyn Thompson

CHAPTER 6

PHONE FINGERS

When was my last day of innocence? By innocence I mean the last day where social media's attempt to tempt me was a failure. The last day I ever lived with the notion that a phone is only to be used for phone calls? When the hell was that? Have you ever experienced those days?

During breakfast I am holding my phone in one hand while eating my cereal with the other. When I am even showering I feel my phone is attached to this obsessive imaginary lease that won't allow it to be too far out of reach. During a movie with the family, even if it's just an instagram notification, if it lights up on the coffee table, my attention automatically chooses the phone. When I am driving even... well you know the horrible answer to that one too. So basically yes, everywhere we go we have this device glued to us. But that's OKAY! I am not pointing the finger I am not blaming I am just saying it for the first time out loud that everywhere we go, so do our phones. It is not supposed to feel like I am bullying you into the corner of the room you are currently in. I don't want to make it seem like I'm gaslighting you into thinking my phone isn't placed right beside me right now as I type this book out for the whole world to read, because it sure the hell is. For some of us we can think back to when the last day occurred that had the "old ways" when it came to a phone, and for many reading this, that concept doesn't even make sense and seems hella dramatic.

Just recently while staying in a hotel with my family I had a moment where I used the hotel phone to call my mother in the room parallel to ours. I had my seven year old daughter hold the phone and I watched her eyes when she heard her grandmother's voice appear on the other end of the banana shaped machine thing. Her eyes lit up in amazement because she never knew her grandmother was that flexible to squeeze into this tiny little machine thing. Well at least that's exactly what her expression was saying. She was absolutely shocked talking on the phone and right at the end of the conversation when she said bye she just left the phone beside her. We heard the continuous beeping alerting us that the phone was idle and off the hook. This alert is to inform you that you don't need to hold onto this phone if it's not in use. This was also another strange thing to experience. She looked right at me and said:

"Was that the phone from the olden days?"

*   *   *   *   *   *   *

Imagine someone approaching us out of the blue back then and confidently saying "From tomorrow until death you are going to grow accustomed to having a lightweight rectangle piece of technology in your palms. You will praise this piece as you may praise and worship the higher power." Now is that extreme or what? If you answered yes to that correlation being dramatic then I challenge you that for the rest of today that every time you go to reach for your phone it is because you are answering a ring. Not a notification, an actual ring from someone in this world who needs to get a hold of you.

So now that we have come to terms with the reality that we have indeed adopted this change without second guessing any potential consequences, it is safe now to take a couple moments to sit in this realization that this device really has this much control over us. I feel like it is common for myself in small talk to bring up the struggles that we face when it comes to phones and the virtual world versus the real world and so on and so on. There is just so much to talk about on this subject.

The world has become emotionless, cold hearted, fake, and somewhat unintelligent. For example, when something tragic occurs, we record it. We don't use the space in our brains anymore to store information and respond in a helpful way, we use the gigabyte space we have in our cellular devices to store footage and share the tragedy of someone else! It is a saddening moment to really write those words out. I say it, and as I admit it, I remember back to a car accident I witnessed on the highway on the way home. Now I understand it is not common nor is it safe to stop your car on the highway and jump out to run straight towards a car that is on fire. But it is also not normal to struggle to get your phone out during a time where it's clear that safety and focus on the road is important. It is also not normal to finally find your phone, swipe over to camera, and try and steady your phone in time to capture the BEST look at this tragedy because, this whole road of cars is most likely capturing this scene, but who captured it the best?

Kaitlyn Thompson

We all aim to be successful, yes. But Instead of waving to the public when we reach the top, we have a habit of demonstrating to the whole world our efforts, choices, and the obstacles we faced on our journey to our successes. This can be motivational and this is the criteria for a lot of social media influencers out there, but have you realized for a moment that success is different for each and everyone of us, yet we look at someone else's and begin to feel a sense of failure knowing they reached "their success" first. If success is different for everyone, viewing someone else's should be refreshing, knowing that humanity is not giving up. Let me repeat that again, once we know that success looks different to each and every one of us, we need to start admiring someone when they reach their goals and feel comfort in knowing we all still strive for the things that fuel our souls. We need to be proud of one another when we see that someone has posted a goal because it shows that we are not just settling for the next software updates but what next big thing we can do with our skills and with our purpose.

If success is different for each and every person, the journey to reach our goals should be only admired by one another, instead of becoming something to compare. We cannot compare ourselves with others and not expect to lose a bit of our own happiness. Even if you are the one who succeeded and you find yourself comparing your experiences to the ones around you who may be doing the same old mediocre thing each and every day, you will lose a bit of happiness with yourself, somehow, and some way. Because when we compare we begin to contrast what we don't have and what we do have from one another and in the end we somehow lose a bit of our happiness knowing we still may not have it all. We are all just humans in a world trying to figure out how we can reach a bit of success each and every day, no matter how little or how large. The importance of posting our efforts and our outcomes are blurring out what we should be focused on, reaching genuine happiness whether it's temporary, or permanent.

* * * * * * *

    I begin to get sad at the thought of this world and the way it works nowadays. Look at me, starting to sound old and troubled when I speak this way. You think I mock older generations when they speak of a love story that sounds like the clip from grease but I don't. They share these stories from the memories in their heads that have reserved space to stay forever because those moments brought their lives the most joy. Instead when I look at those elders I see the confusion in their eyes when I finally focus past my phone and look at them watching me, I don't take that stare because I know it's not that they are judging me, they are just trying to grasp what positives we are getting from tuning out what is actually happening right in front of us. Imagine the little blessings and the inspirational actions of others that could be happening around us that we just choose to tune out while we focus our attention on irrelevant videos and updates from people we may know or not know.

    Imagine the potential best friend that may have stood behind you in Starbucks, wanting to spark conversation because the vibe was there but instead they don't want to distract you from that very engrossing post that has sucked all of your attention into. This perfect opportunity of meeting a lifelong friend has quickly gone to shit the moment you were knocked back into reality when your 'almost best friend' finally got annoyed with you not being aware that it was your turn to get your caffeine order in, nudging you and saying something completely opposite than what they first wished to say.

I know this book may not change much, but I hope it broadens your mind and creates a broader perspective to the world around you. I hope it allows you to accept that we are all trapped in this boat and we are all just going with the flow. This book is to announce that we do in fact deserve to acknowledge our efforts to adopt such extraordinary changes at a consistent steady rate. But at the same token we deserve a small slap in the face, for falling for all of this day in and day out.

I also want to bring awareness to our parents and our parents' parents. Even to the young children. The world is difficult even for the ones that are tech savvy. We are not heartless. We do not mean to record your car accident while you experience your pain. If you were to yell "help help" I know that's all it would take to shake us into reality. We would drop our phones and run to the rescue instantly. I still believe in humanity! I will speak for us all when I say we are sorry that our instincts have changed. Record instead of help. But even despite our response deficiency, with the phone in our hands and our desire to record it instead of really focusing on the situation at hand, I know we still feel empathy for someone else who is experiencing a devastating moment in their lives'. We aren't completely numb, I truly believe we are not completely numb, and I will continue to say this belief out loud over and over again until this cold world begins to defrost.

We have not become heartless with a phone, maybe we have just put our hearts on airplane mode while we allow our phones to take control of how we react to situations and the emotions we choose to express.

CHAPTER 7

CLEANSE

Many people face the challenges that social media throws their way, and we all have different ways of coping with them. I used to cleanse from social media for about a month here and there. This was always such a scary thing to go through and do but I always did it and I always found myself feeling whole again. The questions that you face when you are about to "deactivate" yourself from the social media world are so intimidating. They remind you that you can't come back for 30 days, they remind you that you cant log in, they remind you that you cant see posts anymore until the doors reopen. They really try to inform you of the rules like a popular kid in any typical high school movie who reminds the losers that they can't come to the party. You automatically feel like an outlier in the world when all you are actually trying to do is find yourself again.

I also found myself pacing my own bedroom wondering if I was being a bad person or if It was acceptable to delete someone off of my friends lists. The thoughts and questions of removing someone from my friends list usually come from a place of thoughts and intentions to look out for myself but why did I feel like a worse person just removing their name from my list of friends? The fact that an action that is played out to help protect me has morphed into a "bitch" thing to do makes it difficult to put my needs first.   Yes, before I became more educated on the influence of social media and the effect it had on my personal needs, it definitely felt petty to me to remove them off of my friends list. I mean I have many strangers on my friends list and even family that I no longer get along with too well, and they sit on my friends list so why am I thinking so hard about this one tag name? Why do we question our impulses so intensely in the 2D world? Why do we feel that we can't take someone off of our timeline if they no longer give us joy and uplift us? It is such a strange question that I still ask myself to this day about. It is important to feel healthy about the ones you follow. And yes, even when it comes to instagram or Facebook or twitter, when it comes to your followers it matters who you accept as your friend because they become the things you see the majority of the time.

*   *   *   *   *   *   *

Ever hear that saying "You are who your friends are "? Imagine a timeline full of big booty everywhere and then you would occasionally post a picture of you and your dog. The likes that the peach got was tripled the amount that you and your lil pup received and you wonder how will I ever fit into the world around me? Before you go and change your content, how about you go and change what content surrounds your picture? Do not even dare putting your dog on the ground to take a booty shot!! I mean hey if that's your go to, then by all means go for it. That is not what I want you to get from this example. But if you put down what is most precious to you and what brings you joy just to get the likes that the timeline around you receives, then it's time you change your line. Read that again. Do not dare put down that damn dog! So yes it's also refreshing to clean up your feed and realize that you are in control of your 2D world. Yes, they may have pushed humanity back a couple hundred of steps but we can still move forward and not allow this push us back a few steps and have us lose ourselves in the midst. We can still prosper through life, once we wipe our lenses and regain focus.

This also brings me to the challenges that social media brings to us individually. We all battle some issues when it comes to our expectations on these platforms and the results that we actually get. Many of us will cleanse or clean up or even disregard, but few others will be completely defeated.

My heart goes out to every single soul out there that has eliminated themselves permanently from this earth and from the 2D world out of pure exhaustion and unhappiness that grew from the seed of the Like button. My heart pours out to you and I want you to know I am sorry, and that you are missed.

I truly believe in the afterlife and that concept I won't dive into because this book is not to persuade you to rethink your perspective on that topic if you're not on the same page as I am. Anyways, with that, I believe it is the time where we just take a moment to think of the individuals who were not able to find the beauty within themselves because of the thick smoke that the cyber world can become filled with. A moment to just send our love outward and just grow a larger sense around this fact that people have left us, have literally left their life on earth because they didn't feel fulfilled with themselves not only here but in the virtual one as well. I am so sorry.

I wish that the ones who are reading this book (and maybe for the first time ever) finally feel that they are not alone if they felt they have been the only unlucky one responsible to carry the weight that the 2D world can give. I truly hope that whenever you see the darkness that these apps come hand in hand with, you will not join in on the darkness. You will realize now that you are the light. The ones who are no longer with us, from the bottom of my heart I wish to have one more day with you, so I can tell you in person that you are here, not just in that damn screen and tell you that you are more than a like.

Your life is more vibrant than any effect you can throw on it.

Your story will live on, even past the 24 hours of 'available viewing'.

You are important.

You are not only Liked my darling, but you are Loved.

* * * * * * *

It is the continuous perfection from each person on our timelines at all hours of each day. The posts that portray the good in everyone's lives', those accomplishments and the successes. It is beautiful to witness, as I said this before and it feels good to support and write inspiring things in the comment section of these proud posts. But at what point do we exhaust the cheerleader within ourselves when we feel deeper down, that as we cheer on our followers in the game of life, we are losing at our own game? It eventually becomes too much and we need to pull back from seeing so much prosperity in the world around us during these exhausting times.

Life is not what you find in the virtual world. You are granted 3 lives when it comes to video games. You can deactivate yourself from the hustle and bustle and come back 30 days later. You can have a complete makeover within a swipe instead of going through with surgery. Life online is not life on earth. It will take time to reach some goals that we set for ourselves. Who is to say that the goal you set for yourself today was not a goal user A set for themself 15 years prior? Who is to say that the goal you set for yourself today, and the post user B posted on achieving was actually the most difficult and challenging process that required them to surrender to the disconnecting process with the 2D world just to prosper in the real one?

Don't let another person's post, postpone your dreams.

Don't let what people decide to broadcast trick you into believing that   they faced no challenges.

I am not saying that everyones happy go lucky perfect posts mean that they are struggling before they are uploaded, I am just saying that it is more popular to post about the light rather than what sits in the darkness. Also I am here to remind you that you don't have to feel like you are running out of time. Because darling, you are not.

Back when I was in my twenties and this title flashed through my mind, I knew I had a mission to complete. Like I said before I am very thankful that I didn't rush the process because I wouldn't have so much more to relate too. I wouldn't have true stories to reflect back onto that were actually the results of the experiences throughout the last seven years. The night I envisioned this book was after a shift in an assisted living home that I had poured my heart and soul into. I loved each and every resident in this facility. Understanding the concept of an assisted living home made me more passionate to not only assist these lovely individuals but to try to strengthen their minds and let them understand that I am only assisting their ability to continue on in the beautiful world they created, but because I would be so actively in their lives' I wanted them to see me as a granddaughter that was there to visit and put their feet up on a padded stool. I wanted them to feel as though I was grabbing myself a glass of OJ and on the way to the kitchen I hollered back, "does anyone else want a glass of OJ?" It was home. In this place where I was looked at as a family member from 13 different perspective eyes, I was taught the same lesson amongst them all in various different ways. The one thing they all made sure to let me know was that I had a story to tell. My voice is powerful and clear enough to get across to a large range of people and that this gift should not go unused. One resident himself said these words specifically "You are going to change the world". Sending my love up to him as he guides me through this process today and as I let these words roll off of my fingertips. Also a quick shout out to him just to let him know that he may not have believed it, but his voice plays in my head more often than not. When I doubt my ability. I hear his phrase like a clear and articulate hum. It was within that same timeframe that I realized, my words may get backlash but my words may also resonate with many, and to all those users out there that feel alone, you aren't.

For all those human beings who feel alone, you are not. We are together in this process. Whatever age you may be, wherever you may be on your journey, we are all together. Even when we close our front doors at night, and even when we lay down to rest from the day we just endured, we are still a part of this world. This profoundly, astonishing, and beautiful world.

I don't want to make it seem as though I am screaming for change, or praying that this book is in the hands of the next biggest public figure that has the strongest influence in this world. I am simply just writing to firstly let my emotions run out of my body, and also to just let you realize to yourself, you are really not the only one thinking these things! It is so easy to just ignore the opposing view of these apps, because who really wants to be the one who is preaching about how these addictive social medias are actually bad for our well being? Not me. But here we are.

I just had to let it all off my chest, and you know the irony behind writing up this book? I will log into instagram and I will promote my work on there so I am sure everyone has a chance to see it, if they desire to dive in. So, let me make this clear once more. This book is not in efforts to try and put a law in place, it is just to express my opinion on a topic that I believe I am actually not alone on. I know it may be hard for you to like this book via a double click, but I really hope you enjoy reading the thoughts that may go through your mind, while they resonate with you, through my words.

CHAPTER 8

THE POOL OF FALSE PERFECTION

In my ten year old sons' hands, he holds his phone and his decisions are all based on each one of his precise choices at any given moment. I am in the other room, yes, but he is in his own world where there is a certain "perfection" that will trip him on his chin. Edits that will punch him in the gut. Fake news that will rip away any beliefs in his own dreams. All of those effects are happening to my ten year old and I am just in the other room not knowing he is literally being jumped by the 'influence of a 2D vortex'. It's like he's dropped into a pool of water and he is told that every swipe he does, he is pressing his hands up so hard that his body becomes more and more immersed into the depth of this pool. More deep into this water covering him with self doubt and with the unknown. He is far under by the time he realizes how much oxygen he actually has left. Every swipe has brought him deeper and deeper to a place where nothing is actually fully true. Only way back up for my ten year old who sits behind the wall right beside me, who is literally running out of breathe, who is so far in the social media depths is to realize that he himself has purpose, and if he doesn't believe that himself he won't have the time he needs to push his way all the way back up and break surface of the water so he can breathe again.

I hear his feet make his way to my room and I see him standing in the doorway, he wants my attention. He just had an almost detrimental moment and felt his safety slip away, and all he wants is his mothers attention.

Now assume this to go two different ways:

Most common way: I push my child back into the water. Hey! I didn't realize the battle that he was just facing. Well neither did he! But the moment I saw my son standing in the doorway, I wasn't ready to acknowledge him there because well, I was swimming deep too. So without me knowing the actions I was causing, I just nonchalantly pushed my son back into the water of false perfection. A place where it was becoming hard for him to believe he can reach the top.

The wise way: I push myself up above the surface, walk over to my son and ask him what's up? Spark a damn conversation! Just because I have been watching others' conversations through comments, or videos of tutorials and people looking into a camera so it feels like they are speaking to me, does not mean that having conversations with no dialogue from my end is to be normal and acceptable. I mean if that is the case, I might as well just walk up to my son and swipe my thumb on his forehead until something surprises me or catches my attention.

It is important to recognize that we may be the one who points our finger at one another, accusing this person or that person of being too invested with the 2D world. It is important to realize that while some point the finger at the technology suckers, the other half may not even notice that they too are addicted to this way of life.

That life is no longer about living but about watching others live. It is important to notice when any is completely deep in the waters of a scroll and may possibly need a life saver. These life savers can come in the form of words like

"Hey let's play a card game."

"Want to go for a walk?"

"Let's make some lunch together."

It is just a way to get the attention back from this individual without making it into more than just a simple rescue from the depths of the virtual world pool. I find myself sometimes fully engulfed in the flames that I lit up myself just by trying to simply save my husband from the depths of these waters.

Instead of my innocent idea to do something fun with him I approached the situation by saying "You are always on your phone let's do something instead". These comments most of the time will be taken out of context and therefore direct you to a destination where you find yourself sitting alone while your significant other is cooling off from the argument. We are all dealing with our own relationship with social media, and we are all learning how to navigate with them. Our relationships, whether its a sibling, friend, or spouse will all deal with the waters that my son found himself deep in that day, and now with this chat about how to be more aware of ourselves as we float deeper and deeper away from reality, hopefully we learn to just stay close to the surface of what is actually important.

We are such an advanced world. What is the end game? What are we actually pushing towards? It is so terrifying to realize that some of the inventors of this high tech technology aren't even with us on this earth anymore. No I am not saying that an AI has adopted them and now they moved to another planet with a living biosphere, no, what I am saying is that they have passed away and had a system in place where if a tragedy were to occur their work can continue on. Well I wonder for example, what Steve Jobs would say about the world and how we are using his technology today.

To invent something doesn't mean you're to blame for the punishment and backlash that it may come with. Also I am not saying we are being punished by the use of social media. I am just saying there are many side effects that can potentially occur with the use of too much of these apps. Impaired visions on your personal goals, negative thoughts seem louder than encouraging thoughts, challenges seem to cause fatigue to the point where failure seems more obtainable. Side effects usually occur only when something is used consistently. The one who was absolutely genius to create a belt for pants, to help eliminate the issue of pants slowly falling off our hips and onto the ground, is probably no where similar to the person who decided to pull a belt so quickly and sharp that it would create a negative noise to it that sooner or later we would associate with punishments or whipping. One thing is invented, yet ten ways are created just to use the product in a different sense even if it is far off from the original intended purpose.

* * * * * * *

Kaitlyn Thompson

Let's think about the ones who feel depressed and in this dark place because they are not happy with their own successes in life. If that statement resonates with you, ask yourself this question, are you depressed because you have nothing you feel successful about? Or are you depressed because your archives are not illustrating your success? Another way to ask this question, are you down because you feel like you don't have many achievements? Or are you down because the importance of advertising your achievements is resulting in no one acknowledging the achievements that you are personally proud of? Don't you already feel a bit better, realizing it's not that we are not successful, but we just are not getting recognized through our notifications. Therefore because the 2D world doesn't know what you may be proud of, it doesn't mean we forget to be proud of ourselves.

I had this really amazing woman express to me the difficulties she was facing because she didn't have everything she wanted. All I wanted to say was "Girl me too!" She was expressing to me that she thought life would be different for her at this point in her journey but nope she isn't where she envisioned. All I wanted to say was "I know! Tell me something I don't already know!" But instead of belittling her emotions and how she was feeling in this moment just because I have been waiting for someone out there to prove to me that I myself was not alone, I wanted to make sure that she was heard. I selfishly almost took away her power to express her emotions because I have been waiting for the moment to not feel alone anymore, but I realized later on I can let her know that she is the strongest person to let those emotions roll off her tongue and then later I will say that I have been praying for a sign to show me that my feelings are not as rare as I feel. Two people with this thought can create strength in what was supposed to be a very weak moment. I hope that these words fall into the hands of every person out there who has ever had the 2D world play a negative toll on their lives for at least a minute or so. It is so easy to feel down about others' successes, especially when they filter it, and add in fancy adjectives. My goal with his segment of my book is to express how relatable this emotion can be.

Next time you find yourself posting something ask yourself this:
Who are you posting this for?
Who do you want to like this?
Who is it that inspired you to broadcast this?
Who matters?

If none of those questions has you as an answer, You are doing it all wrong. We don't get qualified to use social media. We don't need to attend social media academy, in order to receive our beloved bitmojis. We don't get a user manual, we don't need to go to the immigration office just to tag a different country as the location on a picture even if we haven't flown anywhere. There is no effort to get into this 2D world where perfection is common and depression is not allowed. We are able to just walk in and either take a seat or get on stage. It's absolutely overwhelming and that's okay. As long as you know it's overwhelming and you understand the importance of getting up and breaking the surface to breathe every once in a while. If that is what I have taught you thus far, then you're already doing better.

I want you to take a piece of this book away with you once you've read the last page. Not literally, but mentally I want you to realize all the moments when the voice you hear right now as you read this book, revisits you in your daily life. Just listen. Because the voice you're hearing isn't actually mine. It is not Kaitlyn Thompsons. Its a voice that you have created, you added in your own bass, your own squeak, raspiness, your own calmness or hectic vibes behind my words, you have created this high power voice box and I hope that when it's necessary and my voice enters your mind, its to steer you in the right direction and to remind you that you are not alone. I hope whenever you hear my voice in your mind, it is because you have wound up in a place where guidance is needed.

I am educating you. Though I may not be teaching you lessons from textbooks, or old wise tales, I am educating you from the life I am living and what I am experiencing through the lens of myself. I am educating you from the bottom. Which brings me finally, to the title.

It wasn't months and months of thinking of this title. Actually this title came first and the book came after and that can be risky business sometimes to try and continue on a topic that was more of a phase but this topic was not a phase, it is my life. I have been through many different situations, I have had many different conversations, I have seen many different lifestyles, and I have witnessed many 2D worlds look completely different than that person's 3D world. I have also listened to many people speak their opinions on this topic. Not just hearing their perspective, but I made sure to not just listen to what they had to say but more importantly what they were trying to tell me. I have even found myself explaining situations to individuals who didn't even realize they were in need of an explanation. I have even spoken the wrong words and I have been told that I was wrong and I even remember reacting wrong to hearing that. I am not perfect. I am a human being with emotions that I work through each and every day. I am not the one that gets #k amount of likes on posts. I am not the one who has a blue symbol that illustrates greatness. Actually, as badly as I want to drop my instagram tag in this sentence just to increase my followers I will not even take the bait at this moment. I am just an average woman who wanted to educate you on what I have accumulated during my time here thus far.

So yes, this is not a reading with many statistics, and experimental studies. This is not a book where I found myself writing, and researching to see if that statement was correct or true. This is not my research paper. This is just a public journal of mine that I am so grateful has fallen into your hands and it's my chance to educate you from the bottom.

Why bottom? Well let's think back to any monumental moment in time. Whether it be MLK's speech, or Eminem in 8 Mile when he absolutely crushed that rap battle, both of those examples held a powerful voice in a very very vulnerable state. It could have gone left or it could have gone right. They both went right. I hope that my efforts to educate you, even if it's from a perspective that isn't as high up on the popularity charts, still leads you in the right direction.

* * * * * * *

This book has been in my home floating from closet to desk, desk to bedside table, bedside table to kitchen table, for the last seven years. No, I have not been creating this book for seven years, but the first day I felt I needed to express to the world that you may think you're alone during those negative moments that result from scrolling too long. You just need to be reminded that you are not by yourself. This was seven years ago. So no, I am not trying to focus on my lack of focus on a project and get shit done quickly. I am trying to emphasize the fact that seven years ago, I was nervous that I was too late in writing this book, because even then I felt defeated. I felt I missed a deadline to a project I was never assigned. I was not too late. Even knowing it's been seven years since feeling like I got a late start on this project, I know that the accomplished feeling I felt when this book was published, was my own success that I reached at my own time.

We have so much power at our fingertips nowadays and yes it can get scary to think of this in the aspect of violence. But the power in the cyber world is endless. The power we have to look like we just dyed our hair purple, or just got new glasses that make us look like a studious person. Or the filters that can make us look like we are literally in bed under the covers suffering from a bad cold, or the ones that look like we are passengers in an expensive ass vehicle, all these filters are fun and make our mind run absolutely wild. Matter of fact, it can also make our minds run right into a huge pool of water where we find ourselves in the same position I explained earlier with my ten year old son. When is it time to kick those feet back and forth with power and purpose until we reach the surface again?

Now let's take this idea and turn it into a 2 way mirror. This is our problem nowadays. We believe everything we see, and we assume there's nothing more to it. A post of a new home owner as they dangle their keys in the picture that comes across your feed while you sit in an apartment that is making your money feel completely dead while you wonder if your landlord in that actual minute is going to knock on your door and remind you that your rent is late. Or imagine a Tik Tok reel of someone trying out 10 different obstacle courses within your 30 second attention span, accomplishing each one and having the audacity to smile at you into your phone screen and remind you that you will never be as athletically built or ballsy enough to complcte that same task. Or! Now this is getting good!! Or imagine being on snap and seeing a filter place you into a room full of guns and ammo and you can see the quick glimpse of how powerful you actually look if you had those in your possession. Imagine falling in love with the idea of you holding a gun.   Now I will just let you realize the meaning of this two way mirror for a second. We see filters, and we laugh or we fantasize or we say ew to the ones that make us look like we are missing 8 teeth. But hello! What about the people out there who actually can't bear to look at themselves in the mirror anymore because the filters have corrupted our minds to play against the gift we were given? What if we fall in love with the feeling of power just by looking at a filter that makes us think of something we never imagined before, owning a firearm? Or what if we couldn't laugh at a filter of "losing 8 teeth" because the filter didn't actually make us look any different? There are two sides to these images, and it's about time we become aware of this idea. Just be aware as you move and swipe and crop and add any effects, that you never forget the first captured image.

CHAPTER 9

PRESSURE OF LIFE WITH OR WITHOUT GRAVITY

It can become so overwhelming to think of the life you live versus the life you project. Or it can be motivating. I heard once from a podcast that you need to ignore your reality if you want a new one. You have to literally ignore where you stand right now and start to envision the way you aspire to be, to such a point that you can feel that six pack under your shirt, or you can jump high enough to dunk the ball, or you can hold enough confidence to walk the runway. You want to imagine it so intensely that you can feel the sweat that it may take, you can hear the ones closest to you asking if you're okay because it's clear your rhythm has changed (a side effect to realizing what you have been doing is not working for you). I actually had a day many years back when I was filtering my children's faces and I just had this scary realization that when I am older and I look back on my pictures of my children, will they all be what I wished they looked like? What I thought looked better for them? Well pardon my language but who the fuck did I think I was? It was from that moment that my filtering went from 100% to 0%. I have to admit though, I make sure to not filter my pictures that's my go to, but sometimes it's just ohhh, it's just so hard to ignore how bomb the family looks with one swipe to the left so I may add a touch on a picture every once in a while, but before this awareness, all of my memories were about to be complete fraud-like.

There was this day, many moons ago, many, many archives prior that I had my own epiphany. I saw a friend I hadn't seen in so long, in 3D that is. I saw this woman all the time via social platforms and she is such a beauty inside and out. Does she fight her own battles? Well don't we all? Does she hold her own truth? Of course. But there was a stretch in time when I hadn't really seen her in this world, yet I hadn't noticed because every time I refreshed my timeline, there she was. Always a sight to see. Beautiful, confident, and a smile so big that I could hear her laughter oozing through her perfect teeth. And then I saw her one day in person. This is the moment when I realized, we all really have different stories to tell, but the only difference is now we have the tools to fabricate and change details on our story, as long as we wish to tell it through the platforms via social media.

When I saw this lovely lady in person she had her shoulders hanging low, her posture was not the one that I saw on her story 7h ago, her face looked faint and her eyes looked ready to lash back if I were to say something about this obvious comparison. I feel like I just described a troll that came out from under the bridge. It was not that bad! But the point is, I could tell that she was battling the fact that she is showing the world her characteristics that she isn't quite the fan of at the moment. Instead of fixing them with results that may take up to 3 months we can just edit and crop and add an effect that will give us instant results. Only thing is, in order to be truthful in 2D you may have to hide in 3D.

You may have to hide who you really are, your sole purpose, your amazing self, your genuine soul, just to make sure that the person people search for on their devices looks like the real deal with no abstract realistic comparisons if they dare cross paths with you via earth.

To dissolve in real life and strive on social media.

It is so strange to think about this all over again now, as I write this out because that day was a big deal for me. I didn't make it a big deal in person, I mean who does that nowadays right? So I waited till I got back home and could really focus on my story and I made sure to add a slide to my story that explained I will no longer be filtering any of my pictures because I never want to be ashamed of the truth. It felt so good to write this out and voice my opinion that no one actually was waiting for, nor did they care about it. Yet I felt it was mandatory that before I go about this new way of posting, I need to let everyone get the warning that you're going to see the real deal from now on. Yes, I would say I was slowly but surely making progress. Now I say that because even though I'm happy with this decision to eliminate filters and take off the automatic effects mode for myself, I still felt it was important to let everyone know of my own changes. But for what? Feeling like it was necessary to post the reason for my actions to a world that won't really give a shit until there is shit to give.

When I say post to a world that doesn't give a shit, until there is shit to give, I am trying to explain how we will repost topics that resonate with us, we will support our friends with their upcoming business', we will repost our children's accomplishments, but these reposts all come with rewards. Whether the rewards are a hug or a discount in your friend's new restaurant, either way, you didn't give a shit until there was shit to give. I am not bashing you, I am making a statement of an automatic response we have when it comes to the Share button. You won't find the average user reposting a meme about a disloyal group of friends when she has the best circle in town. This wouldn't be the case because well, simply that wouldn't make sense. So this post will definitely never have the support of this user's Instagram story because well it doesn't resonate with this user. This user did not give a shit because this post wouldn't have shit to give. If they did in fact post this, they would most likely have an amazing circle of friends that this user would possibly lose.

Back in the day, we know that there were cavemen who did worship and used herbs to heal and all that jazz, just from the markings on a wall. Nowadays we have facebook walls, and we are supposed to be able to go to this place and see how one specific person has lived their life. What do they say, feel, do? We report so much of our lives to an internet abyss where some people will care to read, others will skim or skip and we wait for validation from many different people who mean absolutely nothing to us just to feel what? I ask myself this all the time. I mean I am still learning as I even write this to you all. This isn't a guide, it isn't a research paper, it is just a well overdue rant about a topic that I have needed to get off my chest for a while.

* * * * * * *

My seven year old daughter just asked me what I have been doing on the laptop, and I told her I've been writing about social media, and she said

"I don't know what that is".

I told her she was on it. She has my phone in her hands and has been playing Roblox and when she gets bored of that game she will go onto YouTube and look at reels in her category. Now I really don't want to be the mom who starts speaking about her children and social media, so I just won't. But I will be very clear of the lessons that I teach my kids when it comes to anything with the phone or tablet.

It started one night when it was almost hitting 10 pm and it was extremely late for both my kids. They just had a lot of energy that night and bedtime was unfortunately in the distant future, and I could tell. They had asked me to watch YouTube till they fell asleep. I was clearly over it because I said yes. I know, I'm ashamed. Maybe it's not that embarrassing, maybe it's actually more relatable than shameful but either way, here we are. Then I realized they had put on Ryan's Toy Review. From what I could hear in the other room, I realized this is not going to help with the situation.

"Kids, what are you doing?"

As I watched both of them, eyes wider than the beginning of this issue, headstands on the bed, one bouncing on their knees and watching the screen I realized they didn't understand yet.

"Look look mama, he has a spider man egg and he's going to open it!!"

"You both do know that Ryan is sound asleep right now, right?"

They both looked extremely puzzled.

"But he's opening his toys mama!!"

I could tell they thought I was losing my mind, and that's when I realized that theirs wasn't fully knowledgeable yet. Their minds, were still developing and if I didn't explain this now, they will never live fully in 3D.

"Kids, this is recorded long ago, and right now Ryan is sleeping so he

can wake up and make a new and more fun video for you to watch, but right now at this hour, you guys are only up watching his recorded video while he sleeps and gets more energy to have fun tomorrow"

It took ten minutes maximum for the kids to be lights out, and instead of me running in there and screaming or getting mad that they didn't pick the right YouTube channel for bedtime I realized I can teach their way through this 2D universe instead of scare them from their 3D mama.

It is really becoming a tragedy watching this world morph. I can see it happening right in front of my eyes. I am a part of this negative change as well. Steer clear, I am not trying to be the hypocrite here, we are in a phase of life where being part of this negative trend is inevitable but with awareness of it we can slow the progress so intensely that we can possibly stop inching towards doomsday. Little dramatic? What seems dramatic to me is that I witness every day elders sitting up as tall as they possibly can at their age and observing what is around them. Then I look to the next youthful looking person and they are hunched over with their gaze fully in their phones. I couldn't even tell you where they were in this world. Yes the body of this soul was standing nearby but was his mind engrossed in a Tik Tok from Switzerland? Was he watching an instagram story from Times Square? I'm not really sure where they had their attention too but I did know that they weren't beside me and the older gentleman at that moment. It is a situation that makes me just let out a sigh and I never knew I had it in me to be disgusted with little flaws like this but it's not just about this young person being fully distracted. It is an evolutionary experience. We are in the cycle now.

Give us about twenty more years and we will be in history textbooks about how we first evolved from the apes and gradually moved through the stages of human evolution. Fast forward through the progression of technology and now, we witness our progress, dwindling backwards, back down to where we first began, starting with the first stage of all of us hunched down over our phones and training or spines to allow history to repeat itself.   This will be the new circle of life. We are progressing forward at such a beautiful rate. I have even witnessed it through all my platforms that people are starting to take to meditation and being intrigued with gratitude rather than being rude. We were almost there. But just like an addictive variable, too much of one thing, is never the answer.

*   *   *   *   *   *   *

Let us talk about bitmojis can we?

I want to express my emotions through each pore on my face. I don't want to pour my emotions into a passionless yellow circle in hopes that we all relate, or understand and care.

This has been a big one for me.

"Ayy look at the software update!"

"I already got it, did you see the new 'i'm so over it' emoji?"

"I did!!!! And now I can send it through text and finally make my point!"

E.F.T.B.

We wait, and we wait, till the software update allows us to feel. Do we sit in therapy and get handed a list of choices of emotions to feel? What if we were limited. We want to express this, but we only have that. Just like the Like button. There has actually been a slight change to the like button on Facebook and even this change has got me wondering if I am now an emotionless human being. I want to simply Like it but I should in fact probably hold it down and slide over to the love button because it was really an adorable post and who would I look like if I was the viewer that just "liked" it. Now we are slowly getting more complicated. We think logically, but with emotions the outcomes always become more complex. That's the beauty of being biological creatures. We mix emotions and feelings with logical thinking. It's absolutely preposterous. But it's absolutely beautiful and that's what makes life, life. We put our emotions out there, wherever they may come from, however they may show up, we react and we learn and we hopefully react with more understanding the next time around.

So why hasn't anyone spoken up about wanting more freedom when it comes to expressing ourselves. We are biological human beings who just want to be understood and loved. With all of these apps that take up the majority of our time we don't even realize we pay rent for a home but live in the virtual reality for free. But as we devote our time to these apps our personal biological value is diminishing. I want you to remember the power of really expressing your mind. The feeling of doubt before you allow yourself to speak on how you are feeling. We worry about what others may think, how they may react but at the end of the conversation we feel better. It's healthy to do this and it's natural to do it all the time. Now for our generation and for the younger ones and younger ones we are teaching them they need to react within a box of options. If it's not available on the updates then it's not acceptable for them to feel this way. It's just not healthy. I can also see it clear as day in the younger children's dialogue through texting or on their captions, that being numb is healthy and being vulnerable and real is a sign of being sick with extreme complications. It is okay to say how you feel, and it's okay to not speak on topics that are personal to you via social media. But it is not okay to limit your emotions because you feel you are supposed to.

* * * * * * *

Now I am going to dive into the relationship aspect, of all different kinds. I mean like with our children, with our parents, with our significant others. First off let me just say that I recently just married my best friend, and I wanted to make part of my vows state a line that I haven't yet heard at any other ceremony. "I vow to promise to respect you with my mind, my body, my soul, and my bitmoji". I was so close to adding that in, but it felt like it would be viewed as a weakness instead of what it actually was; me admitting the hard truths. To promise yourself to another person, to have and to hold them, to sacrifice choices for your loves' happiness, to promise loyalty and hone trust forever and ever, it all applies the same in the virtual world. I know you're probably reading this and thinking well, duh. I mean yes duh is a great reaction to this statement. But to also respond to the world and all that you hear like "duh I knew that already", well to know it all, can create the most unintelligent person. What I am trying to say is, what makes you believe what you do is right couldn't be someone else's wrong? Chalk it up, that's it, that's the rules. What you think is right, is right, and what you think is wrong is wrong and that's how you'll move. Well now you've reached a whole new level of naivety.

You need to speak to your people, to your person, you need to make it a lifestyle to want to continuously learn about the people in your life, the ones that you love and respect. I am not saying study them day in and day out, I am not saying if they have a bad day you have failed at this lesson and you mine as well just quit while you're ahead. What I am saying is that, if you and your person like posts, all different kinds, all the time and your boundaries are at that certain length then you will respect those boundaries and continue on without conflict. If another relationship has boundaries that are a little more close knit and you have communicated that you would rather your person not like pictures with graphics containing seductive implications (more or less) then that's where your answer to what is my "right choice", lands. This can continue on and on when it comes to the boundary subject.

What I am trying to say is that understanding who you are in a relationship with, who you signed up to respect and love, comes with intentional boundaries and sacrifices. You need to realize that 2D situations still involve human beings behind these screens. When something is disrespectful online it just lessens the impact of the hit. You may feel a punch in the gut but thank goodness you have a shield from the pain. You are able to absorb what you see, you are able to think about how you will respond, you are given this hard truth and you aren't holding a bomb that is only giving you thirty more seconds, no. Instead the pain we feel through social media can be like a bomb rolling right up to our feet and having instructions on how to activate it. We are in control of when our bomb goes off. We can leave it be, or we can blow things up online. That is the shield I am speaking about when I speak on being hurt through the screen, and the power of deciding if or when you will react. Well, whether or not you let the bomb go off or you kick it to the side and move on, it still doesn't eliminate the pain. Yes, it allows you to react in a delayed response, but if you didn't take the importance of boundaries in the first place.

If your significant other doesn't know the heaviness that sits with our 2D character, then there's bound to be turbulence in this relationship even if you're on cloud 9. Vow to not just each other but vow to yourself to make it a priority, (and if you think I am forcing this subject a bit too much, then make it a 'silly' priority), to be aware of how you portray yourself in reality and on these platforms. You fall in love, you grow a bond, you introduce your amazing self to someone, and you are everything they could ever imagine. They want more of you, all the time, always. Don't let them catch a glimpse of who you are in the 2D virtual neighborhood and want to instantly block your ass. Make it all, make sense, my friends.

* * * * * * *

Imagine Kung fu but each position the fighters hit they can pause the fight and edit, crop in a little extra muscle, then continue the battle whenever they are ready. In real life Kung fu moves fast. You cannot pause, you are only able to use your skill and focus. Once you realize you are in it, there is only one way out, to see it through. In the 2D world, you can hear the bell and begin the fight; you can come across a derogatory post that your significant other liked and commented on, and you can slowly rise up into cobra form, and you can skillfully go through this match, you can take your time, you can calculate your hits and you can hit extremely hard even if in real life you are weak and have no strength. I want you to really understand what I just said to you. When we feel hurt and want to lash back, we have the power to slow it down and really calculate our moves. A mixture of Kung Fu, yet instead of the quickness and responding with skill and focus, you can still win matches by hurting your opponent, and the plus side when using social media is no one ever really needs to know you were down first. This is terrible. These moments of realization, is what I mean when I continuously write that 'you are not alone in those feelings', I hope you feel a sense of comfort during this time.

We create false power behind our screens. Yet with all that strength that we portray, the power can sometimes backfire on us and can really be a negative variable to our relationships. This is why during our vows I wanted to add in that line I previously stated "I vow my bitmoji" but I decided to tell him this in the privacy of our home. I wanted to really explain to him that I promise all of me in person and on the internet and everywhere in between. I truly do wish I did throw that into my list of vows, because this topic really does move me a lot, and I know it would have been something our friends and family would love to have heard and experienced. I mean fast forward almost a whole year since I said 'I do' to my handsome husband, and damn, I have written a whole book on the subject. Obviously it does something to me! And as bad as I felt it was a good decision to leave that detail out, I am realizing that this world is only being controlled more and more by electric hearts and that my vow may have been the next biggest "trend" online for everyone to witness.

I can see the importance of the virtual world each morning I wake up. Each morning when I go through my morning thoughts. I can see how clearly I have been brainwashed and I am so proud of myself to even start to recognize these patterns. When I wake up I start with my amazing stretch, and no I am not about to walk you through a routine I do in the morning and the stretching and holding for 10 seconds in each position and closing it out with prayers hands and 3 deep breaths. I am just going to brag about my own personal stretch that you just can't teach. It's like I stretch my toes as far away from my fingertips as possible andI swear I even grow an inch taller when I stretch like this. Then I hold it and I find this vibrating feeling throughout my whole body and as all of this is happening my eyes still haven't even opened yet. I am just waking up consciously and I am moving physically.

What I just described literally sounds like a freezing cold rabbit, but I promise you it is an amazing morning sensation and once you create some free time with your routine I encourage you to find the most perfect morning stretch of your own and fall in love with this sensation every morning you wake up.

Anyways, each morning, I am able to stay within myself as I feel my body and I can feel how I left yesterday. I am able to appreciate this new day and realize it is waiting for me to make a story of it. After that vibration comes to a slow and I loosen up my body back into rest mode I can feel the warmth under me of my body. The place where I lay and rested for all those hours and I think about what day it is, and what this date entails. I think of the noises I hear around me. "Are my kids awake yet?" I slowly stretch out my arm and I wrap my arm around my husband and I can feel his breathing and I can tell he's finishing up his dreams. I don't want to wake him, and I have yet to even open my eyes. But I am so ready to face this day and I love feeling like I can do anything. I love realizing I woke up. I love realizing I have a chance all over again to be better. All these thoughts are stripped and robbed away from us completely when we dive right into our devices and teach our eyes to open up (not to the sunlight but) to that toxic phone brightness.

As amazing as that morning wake up sounded (and yes every detail is true) I left out the points where my mind would continuously steer me straight to what might possibly be in my phone. I just decided to leave out the truth that when I find myself stretching my toes as far away from my fingertips I am also wondering if I have any red notifications above my messages. I forgot to add in the point that when I found that lovely vibration that means I reached the ultimate stretch right before I loosened up and relaxed again I almost stretched my arm to my bedside to grab my device. I forgot to mention when I folded my arm over my significant other, I wondered if my instagram had stories on it of peoples nights that would be more entertaining that the thought of what I would do with this new day. I just decided to leave this part out because I am ashamed! But I am also aware. I know that I want to grab my phone and check on every irrelevant thing that has to do with the world around me.

I open my phone and sometimes scroll through tragedies of crashes and families that are feeling so much pain, as I stretch and vibrate. While I hug my person, I find myself now laying in the warm spot of my bed, at the start of this precious new day, feeling absolutely guilty to even go through with it. We hold on to so many people's emotions. We see grieving posts and we read their words, and usually, when you are sitting in front of someone who is grieving, in real life, no one is speaking. It is our connection, our spirits that really become linked. So now we are learning to speak about "understanding someone's pain" or "sending our love" as a way to practice feeling a certain power over this topic that we damn well know we aren't ever going to be pros at. Unexpected tragedies, deaths, and something coming to an abrupt end, we naturally have a difficult time when those types of situations arise, and it is okay to admit and it is also annoying to admit. I wish we could just figure out how to be okay with death and tragedies and change, but it is human nature that we grow strong connections and learn to love, just so when we find them getting plucked out from our soil, we are faced with hard times trying to understand what is. The virtual world on the other hand, good thing it created the "Care" button. You know that button located beside the Love and Like button, because it is helping us to feel a little less numb to those actual events that do in fact make us feel human.

I always find myself writing a direct message to anyone on my timeline that is going through a heavy time. I try to make it clear that I am doing it in yes the convenient way, but I am humanly trying to express to them my deepest condolences. I am not trying to take away from people who send out comments from the bottom of their hearts. I admire that and I love love love to see the support. But it is posts like those where we begin to see the invisible wall of the virtual world that separates our reality, really start to dissolve and vanish into thin air. Those direct messages are my way of coming to an agreement with my relationship with the 2D reality. I have created my own rules and regulations. I have boundaries and I try my best to always stay between the ones I put into place. Boundaries are usually set in effort to change a negative result that previously occurred.

Now we all have that one go-to person that really hands out bomb advice and you look at them like they can do no wrong, because they speak about how to do things the right way all the time. In fact, they most likely have done so much wrong that boundaries have led them to being this bomb ass advice giver. They are just talking about their experiences in a more glamorous light. They have been through it, and grew through it and they want to share what lessons they have learned while they are here to share them.

Now, let us go back to the first moments of our mornings. It really does pain me when I think about all the couples who lay in bed with one another or even sit on the couch with one another and as close as their physical bodies may be, they could be countries away from each other. I can't even begin to explain what I mean by this but I will quickly say, one of you could be watching TikToks created in the night lights of time square watching all these people dance in a synchronized way and smiling like they have not one care in the world. The other could be zoned into instagram stories of a group of friends they used to know, sliding through all their stories that give different angles of the same night while they celebrated a night out for one of the group mates. You could be following these stories from your hometown to the local bar to the late night pizza spot that everyone and anyone knows about; all the while sitting beside your partner who is focused on the staircase dance in time square. Why aren't you two together?

What power has taken over the characteristics that you both once before admired about one another? Ever hear of the honeymoon stage in relationships? When everything is too good to be true. When the fun is extremely thrilling, when the romance lingers longer and longer than ever imagined, when everything is truly so perfect that you say out loud "I know everyone says this must be our honeymoon stage but I know with you I couldn't imagine this feeling going away" or "I could stare at you all day". Do you remember when your person was so intriguing you could stare at the lines that form when different expressions came across their face? Or how you can watch them while they watch tv and just stare at a whole person that you just admire so much? With absolutely no effort at all, this person can hold your gaze and attention for hours upon end. Back then we were thinking with our hearts. Now we think with our eyes and we move with our thumbs. Swiping up and up all the way out of cloud 9. Maybe we look at it like an accomplishment. I can sit beside my person all day and we can not say one word but we wouldn't want to be with anyone else doing nothing with. I think we should change this mindset. Communication is so healthy and it is so necessary.

There was a moment in my relationship, months before we communicated and put a change in effect. This time period I found myself asking my husband what he meant by this story he posted, and I would turn my phone around and extend my arm out closer to his face so he could analyze a post that clearly he knew from the back of his hand yet I am showing him like he just discovered a footprint fossil from Bigfoot himself. As I paused his story to show him the words that he put up for the world to see, I could tell I was angry. Let me make this clear, I was not angry at what was posted, but angry that he is choosing to talk and converse with all his followers, while we sit on the couch together in absolute silence. Reading his post, and trying to read between the lines of something that may have taken him .2 seconds to repost, took me 2 minutes to overthink on. I began to feel like I was not just missing his reasons for this post, but I felt less of a partner knowing he chose to tell everyone instead of his significant one. I wish that he spoke that post out to me, as I sat there ready to listen. I wish he would have chosen to express himself to the one who truly cares. Instead of posting his thoughts to his followers, I wished that he would have shared his thoughts with the one that is not ahead of him nor following him, but the one who is by his side, figuratively and literally. Seeing his post from 2m ago on my iPhone while we sat beside each other in silence, started to make me feel worthless. We are quiet in a room together, yet there is clearly so much to be said to the 2D world.

Why wasn't it me that you wanted to express those feelings too?

Who are you talking to?

Who do you want to respond to you?

Why did you bypass me and write this post?

I could go on and on with the questions that rolled through my head. I could try to illustrate what my eyes probably looked like while I hid my face behind my phone. Instead I got right back into the instagram vortex, just to distract myself from this feeling of tears. Why did I feel so emotional? Was it because he posted to the internet rather than wanting to express his mind to me? That was enough of a reason for me. So, in that moment I decided to repost a Beyonce meme that made me feel beautiful, confident, and seen. Within that same moment that I felt so freaking low to the ground, where I felt like an absolute doormat, I made all of my friends who happened to pass my story get this idea that the 'Kaitlyn' in this very moment, was the most confident, happy go-lucky version of herself.

Those two people don't match, damn it.

My whole being, and my virtual being couldn't have been more different. That is the problem with all of us today. How do we succeed in life when we don't even know which one we want to really make as a priority? Do we continue to put all the importance in our image online? Or do we fix issues at hand and guide ourselves through life by our beating hearts instead of by our battery percentage or wifi strength?

Kaitlyn Thompson

It is all about learning, and loving. Being able to learn no matter what age you may be at is really my biggest piece of advice. Once you think you know the right way to anything, you end up lost and alone. I realized that instead of assuming our relationship was going to shit, and instead of believing that he was reaching out for support from other people because my support wasn't good I decided to change the narrative that was playing in my mind. If I am going to sit here and try to persuade you to broaden your perspective when it comes to the effects of social media and how it's important to see life not just through the eyes of our bitmojis, then you better believe I already did my own self work. My husband and I have spoken through so many conversations. Easy ones, hard ones, educational ones, and lastly conversations that proved me to be absolutely wrong. Sometimes we create stories in our minds and we run with them. I mean hey, we are pro creators of creating a 'Story' nowadays aren't we? But when you start to shift the level of importance between our insecurities, our relationships, our emotions, our wants, our boundaries, etc, we begin to place them in the correct order and soon enough we begin to know how it feels to love and be loved in a very healthy 'old fashion' type of relationship.

CHAPTER 10

YOUR BATTERY MATTERS

It was one of my biggest cries for help. Me not posting all of a sudden on any platform. No singing snapchats in the car, no instagram selfies out in the snow, no Facebook status' to give someone food for thought. I thought this was the perfect way to show that there is a red flag when it came to my life. My hormones were out of whack, my mind was clogged with every mistake I ever made, and the questions behind each one —why did I go through with that choice? I had guilt for breakfast, lunch and dinner. I was sad, and I smiled in front of the people around me because it was easier to do, then to deal with the truth.

I couldn't post a smile because it didn't pass the criteria needed for a landing on the Story. I couldn't write about my misery because I felt it was not acceptable. So I didn't make a sound online. I was in a position, in reality, where I felt I was so damn down that someone could have thrown soil on my back and I would eventually decompose. I was crying for help. Well maybe I wasn't screaming for help but I sure as hell wasn't quiet. I was literally crying for help. So what next to do other to mute myself in the virtual world. Do you understand how unhealthy this seems? I wanted to be heard so badly that I decided to mute myself via the virtual world. As dramatic as that last statement sounds, I can bet many of us can relate to what I just said.

I died on the screen. During this time, I died on the screen. Not one of my followers reached out and said, "hey we miss your posts" Or " Hey! Why are you so quiet on your SnapChats? What are you doing lately?" I thought it was reasonable to assume that every one of my followers were choosing not to check in on me because I wasn't important enough to them. Just because I was not as involved as I usually am, I assumed that this change in behavior on my end would not just send them a red notification but it would send them a red flag for my page.

Help her, she needs it.

This is the issue, and this is one of the biggest ones. At what point did we switch our mind and our emotional laws to believe that the users and followers on our social media platforms must be qualified to know when you sense that a follower is in a healthy state or an unstable and unhappy state?

If this situation happens in reality, and I didn't get any check ins from the closest ones around me then I'd suggest it's time to reevaluate the people I chose to surround myself with. For example let's say we get put into a room for 10 hours a day with the same people. We can sing, dance, debate, exercise, anything you can imagine. Now let's say I am always actively involved and then one day I go into this room and I don't speak once or even look up. This is when the red flag is obvious. It is the ones around you that will notice when something seems off. The ones that see you, sit with you, pass you by. It is not the virtual world that is going to notice something is off due to absence because our bitmojis and the robots we use to express our emotions cannot feel to this degree. They can only

E.F.T.B.

Like, Love, Care, Wow, Laugh, as a response, they can not yet "notice/recognize".

*   *   *   *   *   *   *

Even when we are idle, our icons and bitmojis aren't down because they are not needed at this time, they just sit idle with no hints, and no clues on how you may really be feeling in this real world. Ever notice on snapchat when you are writing a message to someone and when the other Snapchat friend opens the chat before you even send it, that you can see their bitmoji pop up out of excitement and anticipation to see what you might be sending? Have your Snapchat DMs always been super exciting conversations or super silly ones? Do you view their bitmoji popping up as a result of excitement? Or do you see them pop up like they are hiding and want you to know your secret is safe with them? Our bitmojis already create this sense of eagerness to hear what is going to be said through a Snapchat DM and I think that is a detail we should all be aware of. This app is creating a sense of eagerness, urgency, sneakiness, all in one, just because while we are typing instead of the normal bubbles that illustrate we are typing, we now grow this more 'human' connection with our SnapChat friend and see that their 2D self is eager for our response.

Then there are the ones that post a cry for help online and it's like screaming on your timeline. Have you ever come across a post where it's basically one of your followers saying I'm signing off for life. But in a very dark way. It is like a post that stops you as you scroll and forces you to just comment on it. Or have you been the one to write up this type of post? I am not here to say you did not go down the right path to getting help. You did not do the correct choice by posting something so dark in a land where everything is cropped perfectly and all dark emotions are frowned upon. I am not here to even shame you if you don't automatically stop at these types of posts to give encouraging words. But I am definitely speaking about a situation I think we can all say we have either experienced or posted and these situations are the most scary. It shakes the truth of the 2D life we live. When someone posts things like:

"It is becoming so hard to even blend in anymore, I can't fake it. I'm   done trying to pretend I am happy and It's time I face my own truth".

This to me is one of the posts that make me say:

"My heart is beating out of my chest as I read their words, and I only   pray that their heart is still beating too."

That's all I worry about. I am stuck in this moment of trying to differentiate dramatic posts, to their usual vibe, to their most recent content, to what should one do if they see someone on the ledge via social media? All of these thoughts and questions rolling through my mind, the sense of urgency to help, the feeling of being completely useless on my side of the screen and then I find myself, writing an encouraging comment to someone who is either waiting for someone to pull them up from the pool of social media, or I am writing on a wall of someone who has already drowned in their sorrows. This is a scary thought and a scary place to be in. This is when social media finally feels a little bit real, when we are reminded why light moments are encouraged; because we all know what dark moments can entail.

But then there is always that Ying to the Yang. The ones who have posted from that dark place, are (thank God) still doing the best they can today. There was no tragedy following their posts (on my timeline). So what? Do I assume that they were being dramatic or do I realize the positives of social media for a second. What if there was a possibility that one of their followers guided them out of that really scary and negative place just through the power of a DM? What If this easy way of communication was used at the most ultimate level of good by literally walking someone off the 2D ledge? If this is really the case, and all these social media outlets via the phone are experiencing better results then the local therapist office then why am I even writing these thoughts into a book to try to spread awareness on the toxicity that lies within the screen? As I said in the beginning, middle, and I'll remind all again in the end, this book is not created in hope to start a movement to try and encourage you to delete all accounts, move off the grid and therefore find the meaning of life. This book is to just vent about all the times when being seen is such a priority, and being seen truly as who we are (flaws and all) is becoming discouraged. This book is to vent about the increasing amount of people who miss what's passing them by because they are locked in on a reel about a laughing dog. This book is so I can ultimately vent in a safe place. This book is to give you, the reader, a moment to realize that you are not alone when you had a day where Instagram seemed overwhelming or Snapchat made you depressed. I am just here to have a meaningful conversation with you.

* * * * * * *

This is why I have encouraged you to write notes throughout these pages, and highlight sentences that resonate with you, because this book is different from all the others you have ever read. This book should feel more like a personal conversation, a therapy session, a podcast that won't lose your attention. If it is cringe to write in a book, then I encourage you to get out a journal and write what you would have whenever you felt the urge to pick up that pen. Create your own notes, write out guidelines for the new boundaries you are about to put into motion, get to know yourself and be okay with what you find out. No matter where this book may end up, on your bookshelf for years, in the hands of someone close to you, goodwill, in a library, in a neighborhood "Take one leave one" library bin, no matter where it ends up and where it lands again this book is all about a good ass venting session. Along with my words and my thoughts, I will now accumulate your thoughts and your experiences as well and this book will travel around to all of us who are willing to put the phones down for long enough to get through these pages.

Back to my cry for help. Back to the time when I thought that a cry for help in the 2D virtual reality meant not to make a sound. Let me backup to the time when I was sitting in my living room and felt that the level of sadness that I had pumping through my veins was actually permanent. I am not sure why on this day I felt as defeated as I did, and I am not too sure of the reason why these days do show up more often than not, but as I write these words out for this book I am starting to realize this might be a good time to schedule a session with my therapist. I am not in a negative state right now, but just because your mind is balanced and the bills are paid, and my energy level is high, doesn't mean all therapists should just quit what they do, hold hands with you and twirl around aimlessly. If I am the one to tell you this then it's my privilege, but it should be more encouraged to see a therapist because the positive side of the brain says go. Therapy doesn't have to be schedules when the negative side of the brain says "hey you really should go speak with someone".

I was in it, in it. I was sitting on my couch and the amount of weight I felt I had on my shoulders made them hunch over. My children would run in and out and ask a question and then run away again. I felt that no one could see that I had reached 'wits' end. They say fresh air, a walk, even an exercise routine, maybe some music, or baking can help lift your mood. I know this, I ignored all of these suggested activities to at least attempt to fix this terrible feeling. Instead I scrolled. Hold on, hold on, I know what you're thinking "But you said you were MIA online". No. I said I did not engage online. I was still fully there, in that room not saying anything and not even looking up. But I was there. Not one follower sent me a notification asking if I was okay since I hadn't posted any activity. Instead I chose to not only ride these waves of negativity, but I was not choosing the quicker journey out of this dark place. I was choosing the scenic route of my pain. I was watching the world continue around me, but not just continue but flourish, look perfect, look extremely happy, successes all around, while I sat with what I thought was my failing self. It was truly the worst way to deal with those emotions that I woke up with that day.

> But it's the moment when the phone dies, that one may realize, they never wanted to.

Let that sink in.

And as absolutely dramatic or intense as it may have been to read that line, I know this will have many of you readers sitting in this moment of realization and for maybe the first time too.

Kaitlyn Thompson

It is sometimes hard to realize how simple an answer can be when the issue seems complex to begin with. I do not want to belittle any person's challenges in life, but we do have a way of complicating situations to a whole new degree. All I needed in my hard times was for the ones closest to me, to say "I am going to take you somewhere". This place could have been a public scenic area for our locals, or a pretty trail about 10 minutes out, or it could have been an ice cream parlor. The people closest to you will know these answers. I suggest you realize who you have in your circle and check in to make sure your best interest is one of their priorities in their lives. Also when you find yourself in a position of hard times, feel free to just grab the reins and instead of waiting for them to give you the directions out of this dark place, you can be the one who initiates the correct path to take, and you can use this new perspective try to navigate yourself to a better place. All I have to say is even though it sounds like a lot of work to travel off the couch into the world just to see if there is something out there that still has some sort of power to make you feel good, it's not. It's not a lot of work and I bet you would have wasted away 45 minutes in that same spot. I am not talking about the couch cushion you chose, I mean you would have been stuck in that same dark hole that you felt you could never climb out of again. Scrolling yourself deeper and deeper into this negative state of mind.

Some days feel so incredibly heavy for us. Some days for some reason feel completely dark even when the sun is blinding. I can't give the answers to why these days show up on the calendar, but they find a way to pencil their asses right into our schedule and we can't call out or cancel those plans. We just have to ride the day out. But instead of sitting on your phone or tablet, whatever form you have, and instead of watching no one notice your pain, you need to start to realize that instead of sitting still in this moment of misery you need to put down the perfect world that lies on your screen, and you need to walk into the beautifully flawed world that you are blessed to experience with no wifi necessary. Don't allow this feeling of loneliness to become powerful enough that you believe no one is with you. Because, I am.

It's very easy to get pulled into such a flat world. Do you remember that "flat earth" era? What do you really take away from knowing that there was a period in the 1800's where many people assumed the world to be flat? Well it makes sense. I mean if you really think about it. It is easier to believe earth is just a flat plane that goes on and on forever than to think it is a sphere shape and we are moving at incredible amounts of speed, and so on. It was simple to just assume that the world was flat. It was safe, and it wasn't complicated. Just like the 2D virtual world that many of us would rather wake up to and live in today. We don't want complicated, so we go to a place where our emotional response is limited, where we can fix our flaws with instant results and zero work, where we can pretend to be okay, when we are not okay, where we can watch someone closely without showing admirable, where we can interact in a happy way, when in reality we are sitting through a day that seems to be so difficult to live through. A flat world is far less complicated than reality, so I understand why living on social media rent free can be more intriguing than paying rent in an economy like today.

The world has become so complex and complicated and so many parents out there feel as though the difficulties that come with their children and technology is almost parallel to an addiction to drugs. Let's get one thing straight, if our parents want to label the internet as a drug, then we all need to check in somewhere. We all need a bit of rehab. We all have this itch to get on our apps and we won't scratch this need until we are swiping down a timeline.

This new era in life, we are all so powerful with our phones and we feel useless when the phone has no service, wifi or isn't charged. Those moments when we feel we are incapable of succeeding in things only because our device isn't by our side, is a form of being addicted to a product and I hate to break it to you, but we are all dealing with this. Maybe many of you have found glamorous ways of explaining why you need your phone actively by your side twenty four hours a day, seven days a week. Maybe many of you feel offended with this part of the book because you think I am trying to plant an idea in your head that you are an addict. That word resonates with all of us differently, and with that awareness I want to state that I am by no means trying to pull up any history that will make you go back down that road of regret, aggression, sadness, and/ or pain. I am just trying to say that too much of one thing is never a good thing. The first step to fixing an issue is to admit that there may be an issue.

Then we have the parents, or the significant other, or the teacher that insists that you get off your phone because you're 'missing everything that is happening around you'. The moment you give in and say fine, I will start Day 1 of this journey and put my phone down, you look around and the whole world around you is using. You realize, if this is my first day in rehab, the environment isn't being too supportive considering everyone is using the device you were told you need to cut down on. You feel like everyone is pushing their wifi passwords on you, notifications are chiming over and over begging for you to give in, everyone is looking down and you feel so out of place because you're the only one looking up now. Oh hunny, it's been an issue. At the end of the day it's not about calling someone out when they say "you're addicted to apps!" It's about spreading awareness and realizing that while someone is telling them this obvious and very common fact, that same person who is pointing blame is subconsciously planning on when they will open up their instagrams next and when they will get their next fix.

Then there are some of those parents who still have the power to make the choices for their kids. They begin yelling at them to be more social and not cheat your way through the world by only having a phone emoji personality. It's easy to admit that maybe we are addicted to this lifestyle. Even when we come to terms with it, we don't necessarily need to cold turkey technology in order to let the addiction go. Rather than cold turkey and letting it go all at once, how about instead of taking something away we learn to add more of something else. Awareness. Once we build more awareness on how much of it we use we can realize where the problem sits and therefore create a bit of change that can create a whole different type of world for someone. So, I am not saying throw your phone against the wall and burn your laptop, but I am just saying there is a placement error on your list of priorities when we focus on where technology sits.

Take some of its power away.

* * * * * *

If any of you has ever felt a bit of anxiety in their life before then the idea of feeling a heavy block of cement laying right across your chest is pretty on point to those beginning stages of a sweet and graceful anxiety attack. This feeling can step in when we think of the idea of missing out on all the news that occurs in the 2D society. The idea of going idle for more than five hours, how would we ever receive the news at the same speed as everyone else? What if someone I know goes viral, has a baby, a dance starts trending, what if there is a world attack and TMZ knew first and posted it first? There are so many questions that will leak into my mind and it will send alert noises to the brain with instructions to go through and check all my apps and to make sure that I am up to date with all the news and hype.

We always seem to go back to what gives us that fix. But instead of saying "fix" I am going to switch to using the term, dopamine. We more often than not, log back in. And that's okay! I am not about to start pointing fingers at you or saying I told you so, I am just having a lengthy conversation on a topic that is well overdue.

Maybe the idea of everyone accepting their flaws, building awareness, and putting the real world back at the top of our priority list will never come true, and maybe this world will just continue thriving off a robotic heartbeat.

Ah, a robotic heartbeat, a life that loves through a double tap on an image, one that expresses their mind through texts and emojis. A life   that will leave behind a beautiful legacy, a story, that will expire after   24 hours.

We are all becoming so numb. When elders talk down on the way life seems to be today, I begin to feel like I am being personally attacked. I feel like the bit of anger that I get from being blamed makes me just want to respond with an evil laugh or something. First of all, I become extremely defensive when someone truly believes that the way I am choosing to live my life is the wrong way. It is hurtful. No matter if your lifestyle is shit or if your lifestyle is something like Bill Gates, when someone talks down on the way you choose to live your life, it just hurts. Opinions hurt until the day you realize you can do what you want with them. For so long opinions and I only had one relationship, I would meet them and I would obey. Now, opinions and I have a completely different relationship. This new relationship has helped me steer my life in the direction I chose to travel in. If I hear an opinion, I don't need to just take it and fold it up neatly and place it in my pocket, I can acknowledge this attempt of someone expressing their feelings and I can check in with my body's reaction to what they said. I can check in with my mental state and see how I feel about what they said, and then I can go from there.

Am I folding this bit of criticism up and saving it for another day or am I junking it? Who is the one who can really tell someone that they are living their life wrongly? Secondly, we are all numb now. We don't even find ourselves receiving notifications with apologies from instagram or snapchat saying "Hey we're sorry for stealing your attention during your kindergarteners Christmas concert". A robot can mop up the mess, yes. But don't expect it to have a natural instinct to warn people to be careful around the wet floor. A robot will just listen to orders and have no sense for others emotions or potential hazards. So when you find yourself in midair about to slam onto your back because this robot did his job, don't lay there and wait for it to apologize.

For many years we have dealt with this gap of having to deal with technology and its extraordinary capabilities as it attempted to seem humanlike, yet there was never really any real human connection. Most recently, we have been introduced to an update that may finally fix the issue of robots mopping a floor with no care in the world about if anyone slips. Our newest improvement within the 2D world is the "Caution Wet

Floor" sign. What I am trying to say is our newest addition to the virtual reality is the introduction of AI. Artificial intelligence. This new character has stolen jobs, stolen the desire to learn, stolen the care to express ourselves authentically, the AI has stolen the show.

CHAPTER II

AI

Artificial intelligence. The magnificent AI. The most beautiful tragedy to occur in the 2-dimensional world we live in. It is truly the most entertaining and admirable equation that has turned into the solution for so many different aspects of our daily lives. People are losing jobs because of AI's, people are lying about their intelligence levels by using answers provided by a robot that is programmed to provide only the smartest of responses. I have seen advertisements, (if you wish to call them this) that illustrated how the AI through SnapChat can fix marriages.

Are you stumped and find yourself not knowing what your wife really wants you to say? Just ask AI because with the AI's experiences in the love spectrum I am pretty sure, that the answer received will fix the problems you have in your very unique relationship.

This new advancement is extremely spectacular and it's also simply terrifying. Like I have said before when it comes to any of the social media platforms, we are offered very few choices on how to respond emotionally. We are being trained to forget the millions of different ways to express ourselves. We are absolutely losing touch on how to truly be present, how to love, how to listen, how to care. Yet, instead of these platforms saying we apologize for not giving you the choice to respond the way you would have naturally; they (whoever they may be) decided to have the magnificent AI enter the world. What do I mean by this? Well just take a second the next time you are in a dilemma where talking through it is the only way to fix it. You have a disagreement with your significant other, your child doesn't understand why you are protective in that certain situation, your friendships feel like they aren't understanding your full value. When a moment like such arises next, I want you to open up SnapChat or your access to an AI and I want you to ask it what they think you should say in this given situation. They will give you a heartfelt answer (ironic isn't it?) and they will give you options on how to express yourself. So not only do we go from a world of limited responses, but now we are blown away by a new character in our chat that has all the answers that we were always taught not to use. It is so blasphemous. It really needs to be acknowledged that an AI is artificial but the intelligence at the end of the day is within us.

We cannot lose the truth that we are more capable than an AI.

Then you think,

"Yah that sounds true but how about we ask the AI to answer a

complex math problem and then ask me. You will quickly see that

AI

is actually genius".

Yes, an AI can indeed answer a complex mathematical equation because of how it was built. An AI can send the exact definition of a term because of the quick access it is programmed with to connect with the internet and online dictionaries. But we are programmed with a thing called life. If in this moment you find yourself leaning more towards AI's instead of the faith in humanity, then this might be a good time to repeat that we are programmed with "a thing called life".

It is becoming so degrading to think of how we have lessened the importance and heaviness that ties in with the word, life. We are not understanding the most important aspects of living anymore. Life and all of its complexities. The situations that can be as simple as asking AI but we chose to complicate them and learn from them and apply this knowledge to the next situation that we find ourselves in. We are living and we are supposed to feel and connect and create meaning to the life we are blessed with having. Reproduction. I mean how beautiful is this word? The power behind reproducing and multiplying your life in this world by adding another life to the mix of it all. Ask AI when they will have a baby. Really expose an AI. Ask AI a question not so you have the answer, but so that the AI has the answer programmed into their robotic brains. I want you all to understand at your own time and place that an AI is Webster, its google, it just has added commas and exclamation points to seem more genuine. Pull down the curtain and realize that answers don't necessarily mean love. We need humanity and all that it comes with. We need the experiences, we need trials, and errors, we need milestones, not just educational answers.

* * * * * * *

So as we can see it, social media is not just a place of the past, it is now the everyday future. It is no longer just a place to log into, but it is a place you need to log out of if you wish to leave. It is not just a space to waste your free time, you are not being granted more free time because AI is slowly taking over many jobs that didn't just employ us, but these jobs occupied us. More free time, more time spent in this 2D world, more time in this world, our 3D reality will begin to evolve right before our eyes.

Ever think about the saying "Meet the Jones'" or have you felt this situation recently? I was just diving into this thought recently about where this saying actually comes from. It comes from a neighborhood where no matter what one neighbor did, the ones closest to them had to try and always have the same (or better). It has become more complex over the years. This certain action is actually a compliment weaved into a sweater made up of pure frustration. It is such a big compliment because what you project and what you chose to value in your life is so admired by the ones who see it every day that they have in fact fallen in love with the things in life that make you happy. They have begun to believe that if they purchase the same items that you own, then their smile will shine as brightly as yours. You are a role model. Yet this compliment can be so irritating and the reasons behind this can be such a long topic to follow. The difference between Meet the Jones' then and now is that, you may have someone who copies your every purchase and action and they may not be your neighbor. You may never have to leave your front door and you might not ever have to wave to the ones closest to you that continuously steal your vibe. They show their respect for you by mirroring all your moves. You may never have to go into your new BMW and wave at your neighbor as he or she gets in their recently bought BMW, same color, same model, same year. It may just be a coincidence, yes I know this, but after about the tenth coincidence it starts being viewed as a "Meet the Jones" reflex.

Meet the Jones' is a statement created by an individual who felt the need to give it a quick label. It can be easy to start to vent about the ones who seem to keep copying your every move and every purchase. It can be so frustrating to watch the ones closest to you compliment your hair color or new sneakers and the next day have the same exact thing. It is just so humane to just feel a bit tense when you're being mirrored by the person especially if you don't seem to tolerate them as much to begin with. Yet, whenever you leave your front door, and you see your neighbor walking out to their BMW too and you find yourself lifting a hand and smiling and waving back. What do they see? They see that you are proud, proud of the person that lives beside them because you two have so much in common.

Meet the Jones' is the label to a situation that is more common than not. Nowadays we have Meet the Jones that live 4000 miles apart. How hard do you have to squint to see this neighborly wave? You don't need to look at all. No one has to wave anymore. No one needs to learn to tolerate the ones who live beside us. We no longer have to smile as we leave our front door, we can just watch the ones we admire, via instagram, Facebook, SnapChat, and we can take notes and mirror the posts we admire. In the 2D society there is no Jones', everyone who lives here in this virtual reality is facing a different "label". Who can be perfectly perfect?

Who can show off their new items nonchalantly?

Who can post a vulnerable state and still have a glimmer of sparkle all   around it?

Who is able to smile so beautifully and big that the picture seems to come with audio of blissful laughter?

It's not about Meeting the Jones' in our virtual reality, it should become "Where did the Jones' go?" The new way we should aspire to be like, is to be more absent from the timelines. This should be the most admirable. It is so easy to find yourself plunged deep into some strangers' whole entire life (or at least the version they choose to show us).

It is extremely easy to be distracted by something that rubs you in the best way and you find yourself stuck on their page minute upon minute.

Stuck in a hypnosis on all the content this person has to offer and you begin to question your life and your choices and why your content is not like this one that you have been plunged so deeply in. Though we are stuck in all of their content, it feels extremely difficult to realize we are diving deeper and deeper into their pool, because their videos and pictures have fed our dopamine beast and rubbed its belly.

Now let's just say as my "chef self" I swipe across this adorable house on the prairie with this adorable chef mama cooking up dinner and I find myself one hundred percent in. I have signed this invisible contract that states I will dive into every post that she has shared with the world and I will try and read between the lines and I will try to find her secret to such a perfect life. This is where we go wrong. We admire and admire to a point where our admiration actually begins to become toxic. It is okay to look up to someone with such admiration and be so proud of this person and still be okay to admit that you don't want their life. Their life may not fit well with the life you have built or want to build. Seeing a page that has a cluster of so many hobbies or items that you love all in one account may start to turn the dopamine you've created into envy and then slowly into toxicity. When we find ourselves reaching that toxic level it can really begin to discourage us. The dopamine levels that are created when we swipe is really such an amazing emotional equation. It really can make our minds run wild with DIY projects and inspirations, it can help us to even remember the importance of imagination and believing we can accomplish many projects and challenges. But too much of anything can be harmful. Build that awareness of the dopamine that you feel within yourself, and start to know when enough is enough. Start to become aware of when you get your fix, and begin to learn how to stop abusing the product.

CHAPTER 12

LIKE COMMENT SUBSCRIBE, OR JUST SPREAD THE AWARENESS

I had the privilege of sitting down and enjoying a coffee with a long time friend. Boy, do I really enjoy this person's company and I think it just roots from consistency and love. First moment I met this individual it was genuine love and care, and to this day, genuine love and care. I remember a part of this conversation, though it has nothing really to do with the topic I have been ranting on with you, I just have to really put you in my shoes that day to get a better sense of how amazing this individual is. This particular moment in our conversation I decided to use hateful words against my appearance, as I began to ramble on about my frizzy hair, and my faded clothes, because well that's just it. Sometimes my insecurities will pull my arms back behind me, tie them together with all my subconscious toxic thoughts, blindfold me with a bandana that blocks out the lovely and true reality and traps me in my dark mind full of my flaws and insecurities. As my hateful mind creates this imaginary poisonous duct tape which will eventually stick my lips shut as my insecurities insist on talking for me.

As I continued on, I realized that this person truly thought everything I said was honestly a waste of a precious 15 seconds that we both will never get back. Also I could tell that those insecurities and flaws that I believe to have power, had no power over them as well. That's just the thing with this lovely friend, it has never been about what is seen, it has always been about what the vibe felt like. Pure bona fide, since day one and for that I am so grateful. Sometimes we meet individuals and introduce our names and give a little glimpse of our stories. Other times we meet individuals and we introduce our souls and we continue our stories with one another included, from that moment on. This friendship is truly an important one for me just because it was built off of nothing more than a soul connection.

* * * * * * *

I was filled with excitement while explaining my plans for this book and I absolutely loved a piece of information I was able to take away from this talk. This is what this book is all about, to just remind one another that we aren't alone when we begin to feel that the weight of this 2D world is becoming too heavy to hold alone. As we were speaking about how technology has truly influenced all of us humans, this individual began to explain just a simple example. When she was a younger girl, she could never resort to sitting on a tablet in hopes to get lost in a world that was not her own. She had to find a way to stay busy and to have fun which always led her to socializing. More often than not she would be with her cousins and her cousins as she said were mainly boys and they played rough. This little detail is important because she stated that it helped her to become a tough young girl, which later led her to becoming a powerful woman. She started with this foundation of trying to keep up with her cousins and the roughness that came with these hangouts. She was able to create a thick layer of skin, not by abuse but by the continuous situations with her cousins that always seemed to test her strength, her endurance, her skill set. She was challenged to keep up and to try. Nowadays when these kids are bored they pick up their iPads or better yet they'll willingly play a scavenger hunt just to find their phones. But that's as far as it will go. How funny is it to think of this. When we have misplaced our devices we don't even think twice about our potentially sore legs or our unfortunate bad backs. We choose to sacrifice physical pain, or holding off on a task, or ignoring the world around us because we are focused on an important mission, to find the missing piece to our being.

I was just placed in a tough situation. As I write this book up my daughter just asked to use my phone for Roblox. I am not here to bash any application or manipulate readers to use an app more or less, I am just stating the situation I was in. As I write this book I dealt with the reality that my daughter is bored, and she doesn't have the brain capacity or desire to figure out the recipe out of boredom. Instead she asks (politely at that) if she can use my phone. I saw this meme once of a mother saying "this is my perspective at my funeral, and it was her little son saying "can I use your phone"? It was actually funny and sadly it was relatable. It made me laugh out loud and also made me realize just by this extremely dramatic scenario that we all can really say to ourselves; imagine?! I mean, really though! Imagine it was to this extent? It feels like that sometimes. So here we are, as I write up a book that you are fully engrossed in, in this moment, and I am determined to vent to you and remind you that we can in fact become focused again, in a world full of distractions, that my daughter is now currently in the world of Roblox. Hmm, I will definitely be putting devices down and getting some fresh air outside when I am finished with this segment, that's for sure. That, my friends, is called awareness!

The toughness that these children are built with today seem much weaker than 3 decades ago. I remember being my daughter's age and playing manhunt outside with my older siblings. I remember trying to keep up, I was testing my cardio. I was trying to be brave even when I was nervous of the bushes and trees at night. I was trying to build a more complex and protective guard over my emotions when I realized that my siblings and friends all made a plan to ditch me and run off together. As I sat on the porch for almost an hour, I was not only waiting for them to return, but I was able to sit with myself. I was able to collect my thoughts, slow my breathing and lower my heart rate, think about what just happened and think about how I was feeling in that moment. I remember sitting and waiting for so long I began to watch this bird fly from its nest and venture off. I was in this moment for long enough to witness the birds return after about eight minutes. I started to wonder if it had forgotten something in its nest, brought back a worm for the bird babes, or if it was just paranoid while being away from the nest that it wanted to just do a quick check in. I was able to sit and wonder if birds truly love to fly or if they are screaming because they are scared of heights. I was also able to realize I wasn't angry at the fact that I couldn't keep up with my siblings, but I was angry that the group collectively decided to ditch me. I was able to notice that I don't have to dislike myself just because it felt at that moment that everyone around me disliked me. I was able to sit with myself, and have a conversation and by the time they were approaching back towards the porch they were all apologizing for doing what they had done. They were explaining that they felt bad when they ran off but then they got distracted with another game. They explained that while they were playing they needed an extra person to make equal teams so their decision actually backfired on them. While I was sitting with myself and taking in the situation at hand, the whole group had their own moments of reflection on how they felt about the choices that were made.

To think of this same scenario but instead of sitting with myself on the porch, I decide to pull out my tablet and start distracting myself with the happiness of the 2D reality, I would have actually been actively holding onto that anger I first initially felt having realized I was ditched. I would have let it build and strengthen as I distracted myself via apps, until the group returned. I can only imagine the outburst I would have had if I saw them approaching as that anger was still sitting with me doubling in size with eagerness to explode. Distractions from issues will never solve them. Sitting in those moments and being open to any emotion that arises is the best start to solving any issue.

It is horrifying to wonder how many kids (under the age of 10) have actually felt what it's like to sit with themselves in an uncomfortable state to a point where they can grow through it. Whether it be anger, or embarrassment, or disappointment or boredom, I wonder if they sat with themselves until the emotions were broken down into a kid friendly explanation of why they may be feeling this. I am afraid to say that many children have not worked their way through situations, they just find a distraction and they use this decoy to feel less angry, embarrassed or disappointed. Later on when that situation is brought back up, we have ruined precious pages in our life story by having to repeat the same chapters over and over until we realize these are the moments where we learn from our situations instead of reserving future pages just to make the same mistakes again.

The other day I had to use the time-out disciplinary act and I had to make sure to emphasize no tablets. It's too funny that if some parents don't emphasize on "no phones or no iPad" during a moment of discipline, don't be surprised when you go in to tell them time out is up and see that they were actually in the world of YouTube reels and vibrant colors and laughter of teenagers doing tricks and obstacles. We need to make sure that the influences of the 2D virtual world don't continuously knock on our doors and disrupt our way of growth, and discipline, as we do our best to prepare our children for this beautiful world by teaching them the importance of making smarter choices.

It is such a beautiful sight to see when we watch young children playing outside with one another. The ages before tablets can be used at their own leisure was truly a sweet moment in time. Watching the encounters and communicating with one another over what structure at the park they would make the castle and which area would be where the bad guys would go, that was their priorities. Watching young children help one another to overcome the fears of the monkey bars or teaching their new 30 minute stranger friend a life lesson on how to just keep pumping your legs on the swings and eventually you will build momentum to be the highest you've ever been. We sometimes get a glimpse of a young child sharing a bit of their snack with their new park friend and in those moments you just sit and watch and live through their effortless gestures of comfort and sweetness. It really is such a beautiful thing to experience and witness. Then the years go by and they become older and older and the children begin to grow a little bit of independence. It is beautiful to watch them evolve, but it becomes a beautiful disaster when we see that they are using their newfound skills of decision making to find the snack blanket and press play to Peppa pig or Ms Rachel while they sit beside a park full of imagination, and "potential stranger park friends".

It's a movement that we are all involved with. Like I have said before we are all just crammed on this boat and going with the flow. No one is at fault. No one is looked at differently when they are out to dinner with their significant other while the tablet is babysitting their toddler. I get it, and I know you get it, and hey this situation may be happening around you as I speak to you through this book! You thought, I just want to get a moment to read a couple pages in this book, so one episode of Blues on the tablet should work. This isn't my chance to talk down on any person's choice of handling the world around them. I am just asking for you to grow some awareness of what we accept on a daily basis and to make sure that we are not exhausting one way of handling an issue.

While we are on the topic of children in restaurants, sometimes we need to resort to a tablet because we have simply lost the battle. But as we are on this subject and I have grasped your attention because I know someone is waiting for me to say the wrong thing or be a "Karen" on the subject, so to say, I am just going to seize this moment. Instead of pulling out the tablet as option number one try to look up easy ways to entertain your child in a restaurant setting. Many times restaurants have packets of crackers, oyster crackers for example, and this bag is one of those satisfying sounds and textures that young ones can't get enough of! Also many restaurants have crayons and paper for children, but if they are too young for crayons (still at the stage of should I draw or eat the purple?) then you can always distract your child by drawing a simple picture for them. You never know how intriguing it can be to realize mama or dada drew a tree! Also if you are out at a restaurant and you want to avoid the tablet for as long as possible, bring some table top friendly toys. Make yourself a little toy chest for restaurants by using a lunchbox and always having an easy to grab bag of restaurant friendly toys that you can always pack with you and let your child dive into. My most favorite and fascinating toy I see so much lately are the water brushes that just get the picture wet and the colors pop out of nowhere when the paper is damp. It is such an amazing distraction method in a restaurant and it's intriguing to even adults (me). So now that I am done promoting some quick products and easy ways to distract your children while at dinner, instead of pushing them into a 2D virtual world first, how about resorting to that last and having fun with those new options I have just described.

I aspire for this book to feel as real as any non glamorous life situation. For example, an encounter with someone at a coffee shop. I'm not just talking about a bistro or a beautiful boutique on the corner with espressos, croissants and a pretty vine backdrop. I'm speaking about this book being as real as an encounter you could have during the mad morning rush at the Dunkin' Donuts drive thru. Imagine the line being extremely long that you find yourself debating on sipping this delicious coffee with no job or just leaving the line and not getting fired for being late (and getting to work with no coffee). This book is as real as the moment you pull out of this commitment of a line and pass by a person like me as you roll your window down and yell

"What is this shit? "

As I smile and roll my window back down to say:

E.F.T.B.

"I honestly don't know what the hell is going on but I need my iced latte asap because I just got my nails done and I need a prop to hold while I post these beautiful creations on my story".

I am trying to make this book, that real. As dramatic as that scene may have seemed as it played out in your head, this world is just the same. Every situation has either been amplified, or put to an extreme hush. I am here to write out all that we know, and all that we didn't realize we knew.

This book is as real as me admiring that I had asked my mother to proofread before posting it online. This book is so real that if there may be mistakes found within the pages you could hopefully be compassionate and understanding at the fact that humans do make mistakes. This book is so real that you may wonder if my mom critiqued this book by changing it to what fits better with her perspective or if she just read the words and corrected grammar. Well in fact, she did take the initiative to read over my work and I was curious as to what she thought "correcting my work" actually meant. I loved that when I received the book back it wasn't morphed into her perspective of the influence of the 2D world, but she was able to listen to me and I felt that not only was my work edited, but I was also heard.

It's not just that I was heard on this topic, it was just so much more than that. I'm not talking about just the apps and the descriptions of each one and what they are designed to do. I'm not speaking about the 'genius' who created them and how they understood what can increase dopamine while also distracting us from the harsh realities. I am here to talk about what life has become. When my mother proofreads this book, she was able to read what her daughter's life has become. It was finally clear that even though the younger generation is tech savvy, may understand the buttons more, may understand what filter works best with this type of sunlight, it does not mean that we want this. I finally felt a huge wall crumbled to the floor and it didn't just fall, but was crushed with so much force it just turned to pure dust. All we have to do now after having spread this awareness to the world, is to allow the dust to settle, and continue on.

I started this book in 2017 and I love that I took it as a priority to document the start date to this project. I knew that I wanted to create a book, and I knew that a timeline with this certain goal, would make my goal feel unattainable rather than realistic. If I say I will do something within this given time, I try for a bit then I will realize that life isn't about rushing to results.

Now isn't that the most graceful excuse you've ever seen? Anyways, despite the length of time between my start date and my publishing I am proud of myself for understanding the goal that I had, and choosing to value and experience the years in between. Those years were crucial moments that allowed me to "take research, create stories, filter pictures, deal with drama via comments, Like things, create subliminal messages, cry, learn to let go of a follower or two, learn to add the followers that actually add value to my life, to my lifeline, to my timeline.

I have also realized that as I created this book through the lens of myself, Kaitlyn Thompson, I realize that it is okay to have readers disagree, or question an assumption I have made about the impacts of social media platforms on our reality. I am eager to hear responses from readers from all over on how they feel after diving into this book with me. In my opinion , as I've said in the beginning, this is not a book to encourage an abrupt stop in using technology, or a march for change, I am writing this book to simply vent, to make it clear that your feelings are not as unique as you may feel, and that we are not alone when it comes to the struggles we face with these platforms. I am here to create a moment to encourage you as an individual in this very advanced world to have more awareness of the impact of opening an app, and of expressing yourself through only a limited amount of options. Even reading this book has guaranteed potentially 3 hours of your time, and that for myself is a success within itself.Just being able to think for a moment, from a whole different angle than usual is an accomplishment within itself. We open our phones, we scroll through our comments, we post a picture to stay within the hype of things online and we do it without a true desire anymore. We have created this type of muscle memory within our "thumbs'" as you would say, where we feel as though we need to keep this unwritten rule of announcing all that occurs, every single bit of it, as long as it doesn't fall too far out of the criteria for social media acceptance.

* * * * * * *

So, what really happened to just living by choice? Our choices went from a full range of options, to slowly becoming seldom to none. Become aware that our freedom to make our own choices is fading. Let's make our power strong again. Let's make it a goal to bring back the importance of deciding. When was the last time you found yourself caught in the rain? Has it occurred lately or do you choose to check your phone for the hour by hour answers for what the sky is feeling like?

Let me challenge you to make the choice to just go with the wind. No pun intended. Don't choose to always know. It's okay to be caught by surprise, it is okay to not always be one step ahead of the game. Start to rediscover the beauty of the unknown. Tell yourself that today you will do less with the 2D reality and more with yourself.

Take your focus away from the timeline and add more value to your lifeline. We don't always need to double tap or receive a double tap from someone in this world just to know that life is good. Life has become so simple, so convenient when it comes to technology that this simplicity is transforming life into a numb, messy and useless disaster. I may never know if the person who is reading this is famous, 'instagram' famous, or has 10 followers to their name, but I do know that right now as I speak with you and you've spent time with me in this book, that you know you have a beautiful life, and you're eager to rediscover it.

* * * * * * *

E.F.T.B.

Kaitlyn Thompson